"Sherrie Campbell has written a must-read for anyone [...] family members. Her book brings together the critical ele[...] overcoming childhood shame, and guides her readers thr[...] healing while helping them create self-empowering boundaries. Each chapter of her book offers profound insights into the most common struggles faced by adult survivors of toxic family dynamics."

—**Kim Saeed**, author of *How to Do No Contact Like a Boss!*

"Sherrie Campbell has written a number of must-read books on dealing with toxic family members and loving yourself in the aftermath. Her latest book is yet another gem that will resonate with anyone seeking support for overcoming toxic relationships. Her book is a must-read for mental health professionals because this area of trauma is too often ill-informed and misunderstood. Read this book and connect with Campbell on social media for knowledge that will help you thrive!"

—**Dan Pierce**, founder of Mentally Fit, and Thrive Global contributor

"Until I read this book, no self-help book had enabled me to cut ties with my toxic family, or to heal and deal with the aftermath. I followed Sherrie Campbell's blueprint step by step. Her work eased the lifetime pain in my soul in weeks. This book is helpful for survivors of this type of trauma, and also the clinicians who come across this topic in their office. This book brought me back to my estranged father to receive forgiveness before he died, and discover a shocking truth I never knew. I can only describe what occurred as a supernatural event. I was an emotionally broken child and a self-worth chaser. I am now a perfectly broken adult, with secure boundaries in place, more emotionally mature, and I know I am enough."

—**Tom Dutta**, award-winning Canadian CEO, international best-selling author, TEDx speaker, and radio and film producer

"With compassion and empathy, Sherrie Campbell's words wrap around the reader, providing a clear guide to authentic healing from toxic relationships. Campbell weaves vulnerable vignettes of her experiences as a woman who decidedly exited a toxic environment, and openly shares them. She offers readers guidance while providing missing puzzle pieces. She demonstrates that it is possible to be free of a haunting, toxic family and live a fulfilled life centered in peace. I highly recommend *Adult Survivors of Toxic Family Members* to those who desire true freedom moving forward in their lives."

—**Julie Lokun, JD**, masters certified life coach and facilitator of dreams at Crown & Compass Life Coaching, LLC

"Sherrie Campbell offers a unique and true-to-life view of what it means to separate yourself from toxic family members. She clarifies what toxic family abuse is, the impacts it has on creating lifelong feelings of shame and confusion, and she gives the reader practical steps to heal their lives, so the abuse stops with them. Campbell isn't just an expert, but also a survivor, which makes her more relatable to those who are living through this type of pain. Campbell believes that readers coping with this type of trauma often need another survivor more than an expert to truly understand the complexities of moving away from toxic family abuse. In this book, you are given full permission to feel what you were never allowed to feel or speak about."

—**Jack Canfield**, coauthor of the *Chicken Soup for the Soul®* series and *The Success Principles*™: *How to Get from Where You Are to Where You Want to Be*

"Before interviewing Sherrie Campbell a couple of years ago, I innocently said, 'It must have been so difficult to choose to cut your family out of your life.' To which she quickly responded, 'It wasn't a choice, it was something I had to do to survive.' This was an 'aha' moment for me. Campbell, through her expertise and personal knowledge, guides those who are experiencing toxic family pain and offers them a practical path to heal, survive, and ultimately thrive. As a survivor herself, Campbell is the perfect voice to help individuals who are suffering from this unimaginable familial trauma and shame, and gives them permission to set lifesaving boundaries to break free. I look forward to recommending Campbell's newest book, *Adult Survivors of Toxic Family Members*."

—**Robi Ludwig, PsyD**, TV personality, psychotherapist, and author

"Sometimes the healthiest thing to do is practice firm boundaries with toxic people, even if it's with your family. Sherrie Campbell uses compassion, her expertise, and a direct approach in this book to change your life forever. It contains a wealth of information about toxic family members, and will give anyone who reads it incredibly helpful knowledge on how to prepare mentally and emotionally to go no-contact with family members, grieve the loss of these relationships, and maintain healthy boundaries. From Campbell, we can all learn that healing the wounds of misunderstanding comes not from getting others to understand you, but from having the courage to stand alone against all odds."

—**Julie Hefner**, author of *Nourishing Your Body and Soul*

Adult Survivors

of

TOXIC

Family Members

tools to maintain boundaries,
deal with criticism, *and* heal from shame
after ties have been cut

SHERRIE CAMPBELL, PhD

New Harbinger Publications, Inc.

Publisher's Note

This publication is designed to provide accurate and authoritative information in regard to the subject matter covered. It is sold with the understanding that the publisher is not engaged in rendering psychological, financial, legal, or other professional services. If expert assistance or counseling is needed, the services of a competent professional should be sought.

Distributed in Canada by Raincoast Books

NEW HARBINGER PUBLICATIONS is a registered trademark of New Harbinger Publications, Inc.

Copyright © 2022 by Sherrie Campbell
New Harbinger Publications, Inc.
5674 Shattuck Avenue
Oakland, CA 94609
www.newharbinger.com

Cover design by Amy Daniel

Acquired by Elizabeth Hollis Hansen

Edited by Kristi Hein

All Rights Reserved

Library of Congress Cataloging-in-Publication Data on file

Printed in the United States of America

24   23   22

10   9   8   7   6   5   4   3

To my lovely daughter, London.

You are my "why."

I love you.

Contents

Foreword

Some of the most challenging issues in psychotherapy are, unsurprisingly, linked with the distressing experiences endured by someone who is dealing with the toxic effects of an abusive partner, parent, or family member. The emotional suffering can be intense and dysregulating, experienced as states of hopelessness, depression, unremitting worry, or anxiety. As part of the survival system, you may find yourself, at times, shifting into maladaptive patterns of self-doubt and self-sacrifice: forfeiting your needs, muting your joy, losing your grip on an otherwise sturdy internal self-advocate, weakening your confidence, and compromising your most authentic voice.

As an expert in narcissism, it is not unusual for me to meet partners and family members who have been plagued by acts of betrayal, abuse, neglect, subjugation, gaslighting, disregard, control, and contempt. Living in a toxic family where non-negotiable borders are constantly being violated can set the stage for the human survival system to launch coping reactions, such as enmeshed loyalty at all costs, submission to unrealistic expectations and burdens, self-sabotage and subjugation, intense anger, or intense inhibition of feelings. These maladaptive patterns are formed early in a child's core development—when emotional needs are not adequately met and noxious experiences construct the framework for a child's self-concept (along with biology and temperamental makeup)—to become the lifelong automatic responses to ongoing familiar and familial threats.

Therefore, I could not be more delighted that my colleague, Dr. Sherrie Campbell, has written this extraordinary book. In *Adult Survivors of Toxic Families*, her voice is clear, beautifully eloquent, and thoughtfully metaphoric, coming from the wisdom of lived experiences both personally and professionally. Sherrie gives us a raw and gracious glimpse into her own personal life challenges, inclusive of poignant struggle and resolute strength, while sharing bold and essential strategies for healthily adapting and recalibrating the embedded biased messages and emotionally warped thought patterns that arise from repetitive exposure to damaging life scripts. Sherrie reminds us that no family is perfect and that painful family issues can remain with us long after the actual interactions have happened. She shows us that while strife and disagreement are part of human interactions, we must employ critical discernment between typical negotiable conflicts and unsustainable toxic relationships where boundary-setting is mandatory for emotional health and well-being.

This book assists in the art of limit-setting: rethinking and reassigning the frequency and proximity of contact with toxic family members. By brilliantly shining light on the most powerfully relevant issues and painfully hard-held secrets that so many suffer with and endure throughout their lives, Sherrie invites you to open a door to a world where your grief can be embraced and carefully processed. It is a world where you might not have to keep "fetching your heart from the lost and found" and where you can finally take the "pen in hand to be the author of your own life."

Sherrie has devoted years to her clinical practice as an expert, consultant, and psychotherapist, with several previous books. Now, in *Adult Survivors of Toxic Families*, she provides an incomparable guide that will not only resonate with both your lived and prevailing experiences, it will offer effective healing strategies for those longstanding and profoundly engraved emotional wounds that continue to echo within the walls of your emotional memory. These are strategies that can transform destructive life patterns into healthy, sustainable ones.

I confidently recommend Dr. Campbell's book as an invaluable resource for anyone who is dealing with the ongoing challenges of toxic family ties or with the aftermath of a toxic relationship that has been ruptured. *Adult Survivors of Toxic Families* will light the path to emotional emancipation, to a reawakened and renewed sense of empowerment...to exhaling again.

—Wendy T. Behary
    Author of the international bestselling book
    Disarming the Narcissist

Introduction

You Have Permission

The decision to sever ties with family is a commitment of body, mind, and spirit. Setting no-contact boundaries, or something like no contact, requires blind faith that you will be better off apart. *No contact* is a prohibition of direct or indirect contact of any kind—physically, verbally, or anything in writing—between yourself and another person or group. This decision must be made with the belief that choosing to go through life without your family means you will not just be okay; you will be better than okay. Your definition of "okay" may be different from what you had hoped or initially envisioned, but I assure you, feeling healthy and happy is absolutely possible under these circumstances.

The no-contact boundaries I will help you set and maintain in this book can create the emotional and mental safety you have needed your entire life. These boundaries can bring you the relief from family pressures that you have long sought to feel. These boundaries are strong enough to provide protective armor against your perpetrators. With boundaries in place, you can be free to live your life, out from under the constant abuses, scrutiny, dramatics, and manipulative games of your toxic family system.

Still, as I experienced, cutting ties with family has two competing emotional sides. On the one hand, it is completely liberating. We can feel proud that we finally took a stand for our rights to be loved for exactly who we are. On the other hand, there is a certain undercurrent of self-doubt and toxic shame that plagues us as we move forward alone, wondering if perhaps we are doing something horribly wrong.

Why? Because it is our family. Who does not need or want a loving family? We all do.

Unfortunately, the system in which psychologically abusive family members act refuses to accept any way other than its own. There is only one way in a toxic family. Toxic family systems are not open to change, different ideas, or flexibility of thought or person. For us, tolerating their way turns into acquiescing to their abuses. Acquiescing goes directly against healthy development of the individuality, freedom, love, and happiness that we have a right to seek and deserve to find.

Toxic family dynamics are largely based in the *groupthink* paradigm, wherein all thinking and decision making within the family system strongly discourages the creativity, independence, or individual responsibility of each family member. A toxic family system works because it is strong in numbers, which is powerful when the method of intimidation is ganging-up warfare and you are an innocent child. You have been groomed with this type of intimidation from your earliest days.

As a doctor, researcher, learner, and healer, I cannot see how staying connected to a system that discourages individuality or individual responsibility can lead anyone down the path of truly knowing, creating, and embracing who they really are. Self-worth has likely become an elusive concept that you long to experience and discover but cannot seem to achieve, because your family system provides no option for you to naturally separate and individuate from their clutches. This must happen for you to be able to define your self-worth.

In my experience of finding my way out of an abusive family dynamic and healing my own life, I found that most information I sought to help guide me didn't encourage or suggest the option of severing ties. Most of it educated me on understanding what toxic was, the different types of toxic people, the varying impacts toxic family members have on us, and how this toxic system influences how well we function in the world. While the information I read and researched did add tremendous value to my growth, little of what I found gave me the permission I needed to take care of myself wholly and fully. Further, no one could answer the questions I asked myself privately as I was unpacking my trauma, because the literature teaches us that staying connected to family, to at least some degree, is an integral part of the solution to our pain.

Problem is, I knew that if I tolerated abuse on any level, I would continue to be abused. While staying connected to a psychologically abusive family may be possible for some, many of us know that staying connected is exactly what will not allow us to grow and become healthy people.

It would mean continuing to live as the shut-down, fearful, abuse-tolerant, victimized version of who we are. How is this good for anyone? I lived this way for years, and the research fell far short of helping me heal and cope. Perhaps you're like I was, convinced of the need to be a "good person" by maintaining some contact with a toxic family. Yet that "good person" version of you was being totally inauthentic and harmful—not to the family, but to yourself. To be a "good person" means you stay close enough to still be abused.

It can take years to finally cut ties, because we have no idea what could happen to us or our lives afterward. The thought of that unknown, living life all alone, is dark and terrifying. For me to be brave enough to push forward in my own healing, I needed to feel like someone really understood my pain, my internal conflicts, and my fears. I wanted and needed to see how someone like me felt going through the process of severing ties with family, and what challenges or conflicts they faced when making decisions. This is why, in this book, I include my story—which has been both liberating and terrifying.

In the journey of healing in the aftermath of cutting ties, I have felt like a lone trailblazer. I have had to live and walk this path blindly; however, I now know the way through, which gives me something special and valuable to offer all of you who have experienced the same gaps in the research.

I firmly believe we cannot heal while we are tolerating abuse. This is why I and many others choose the option of no contact, which I wrote about in my 2019 book *But It's Your Family: Cutting Ties with Toxic Family Members and Loving Yourself in the Aftermath*. I address the aftermath of cutting ties, because when people hear the words "cutting ties" or "no contact," they may automatically assume those who cut ties are angry, bitter, immature, spiteful, spoiled, jealous, entitled adult children who are being cruel and unreasonable toward our family members. Nothing could be further from the truth. Cutting ties is not about malice, hate, stubbornness, a lack of forgiveness, being spoiled, or exacting revenge. Severing ties is exclusively about self-care.

I do not write about this topic to break up families. I cannot fracture a family that is already toxic and broken. My intention is to bring light to this important topic and offer healthy, practical options for self-care. In my view, cutting ties is largely about keeping families together in the generations to come—after someone like you or me decides that the family abuse stops with us.

There is hope and clarity to life after cutting ties with toxic family members, and in this book I will illuminate both the opportunities and the challenges. The habit of not trusting yourself has been programmed into you from a young age. This lack of self-trust has made it incredibly challenging for you, as a survivor, to take the necessary steps to protect yourself. This same lack of trust can seem like a slow bleed as you continually wonder whether you have made the right decision, or when you feel unfairly judged and criticized by a society who cannot fathom anyone needing to decide to sever ties with their family. Because you were raised to be and feel insecure, it's no surprise that you question whether you are too sensitive or too harsh with your boundaries. I know that healing this self-doubt is critical to living a fulfilling, joyful, and love-connected life. In the aftermath, you have the opportunity to make sense of all the confusion, guilt, anxiety, loneliness, and sadness. All the antidotes and the skill set provided in this book offer you new boundaries to set and new ways of thinking to adopt.

When you establish no contact with toxic family members, the greatest gift you give yourself is the uninterrupted time and space to repair your core wounds, to start recovering truly and deeply. Your core needs start at birth and must be met. Core needs for children include, but are not limited to, receiving adequate levels of time, love, and attention, along with meeting their needs to feel heard, validated, and understood. When these needs aren't met, there is no way to rewind to the beginning of life in a way that enables any outside love relationship to heal or meet your core needs. Research naively suggests we seek other relationships outside our family to supply our basic needs of love, acceptance, and emotional support. Although other love relationships are fundamental, necessary, and important to our overall well-being, I believe it is not only inappropriate for us to put this type of pressure on others to fill the needs our family neglected, but this request is also impossible to satisfy. It is unwise and emotionally dangerous to assume anyone could meet the core needs that can be met only by the family we were born into. The unfortunate message from this type of information is that other people can heal our wounds and meet our core needs when, ultimately, we need to learn to heal our own wounds and meet our own needs.

Healing comes through an intimate examination of what you have lived through in the past and how it has led you to this point. The most important work you do as a human being is the work of reclaiming your life. My sole—or soul—intention is to help you embrace and maintain your healing momentum. I will share some of the unexpected bumps in the road of the aftermath that I and others have encountered, and provide a road map on how to stay committed to self-care without looking back. Your destructive family needs no role in the recovery process. The best recovery is the one you earn on your own. I give you permission to do the following:

You are allowed to terminate relationships with your toxic family members.

You have permission to walk away and be done with any person who is consistently harmful to your well-being.

You have permission to feel and be angry, to take care of yourself and your needs, and to not be naïve with offers of forgiveness.

You have permission to take care of your life in any way you choose without having to explain your self-care decisions to anyone.

To remind yourself of this whenever you need to, download this online free tool from http://www.newharbinger.com/49289, print it, and post it anywhere you want.

PART 1

making *peace* with your decision

Chapter 1

Understand That Severing Ties
Is Self-Protection

When you sever ties, you do so for your own protection and emancipation. Severing ties is not intended to cause harm, hurt, or upset to your family members. When you make a decision such as this, nothing is being done *to* your family members by you; rather, you are doing something essential *for* yourself. Yet this emancipation will not be all roses and pixie dust. It unavoidably has its own ugly and painful side, so above all remember that you are doing this to take care of yourself.

There are common reasons we feel the need to sever ties with family members, whether it is cutting ties with parents, siblings, grown adult children, or other extended family. Ironically, these reasons do not vary much from the same reasons you would cut ties from a toxic friend, partner, or coworker. Here are some common reasons you may have already cut ties with your abusive family members—or want to:

- Emotional abuse and manipulation, including things like rewriting history, gaslighting, lying, smear campaigns, projection, triangulation, deflecting, blaming, shaming, ostracizing, guilting, drama, love-bombing, hoovering, spying, invasiveness, controlling, or being impossibly argumentative

- Financial abuse

- Physical abuse

- Sexual abuse

- Addiction and neglect

- Different or conflicting values

- Poor boundaries

- A general lack of respect

- A lack of loyalty and honesty

- Ganging up, as when one person is ostracized by the entire family

- Gossip

I hope you feel some relief as you read through the common reasons many people choose to cut ties with their family members. These are the whys of the process. These let you know you are not alone. Luckily, the whys are much easier to assimilate than the hows, because the hows require that you take action—which, in these types of emotionally charged situations, inevitably creates fear and anxiety. The following are useful ways to let your family members know you will no longer be in touch with them, establishing no-contact boundaries:

- Have a conversation (knowing it will be nonproductive).

- Write a letter detailing your decision.

- Pull back without explanation.

- Go no contact. Block. Remove. Delete.

Moment of Insight: There is no perfect way to sever ties. What matters is that you sever them if you need to.

Take a Moment for You: Consider how it works best to sever ties in the least hurtful, easiest way for *you*—knowing it will be doable, though not necessarily conflict-free. Write down the ways you are taking this action to take care of yourself. What, specifically, are you protecting yourself from? What behaviors will be forced out of your life? In essence, write down how you will benefit from cutting ties. Then keep these responses in mind as you go through this book's process of removing your family's negative influence from your life.

Defining Traits of Toxic People

To understand toxic family members more fully, it is important to examine the defining traits that qualify a person as toxic. I prefer the word "toxic" to the labels or diagnoses given in the *Diagnostic and Statistical Manual of Mental Disorders* (*DSM-5*). The term "toxic" offers a simple way to sum up an individual who expresses multiple traits from the varying Cluster B Personality Disorders in the *DSM-5*. By identifying the defining traits of your toxic family, you gain more insight into who and what you are dealing with. These traits show you that they are, in fact, toxic by diagnosis, not as a result of your imagination or sensitivities, as your family members would like you to believe. It's likely several of the following traits describe each individual:

- Is uncomfortable unless the center of attention

- Displays rapidly shifting emotions

- Acts very dramatically

- Is overly concerned with physical appearance

- Constantly seeks reassurance or approval

- Is excessively sensitive to criticism or disapproval

- Has a low tolerance for frustration

- Makes rash decisions

- Has difficulty maintaining relationships, often seeming fake or shallow

- Threatens or attempts suicide to get attention

- Exaggerates achievements and talents

- Believes they are superior

- Monopolizes conversations

- Expects special favors and unquestioning compliance with expectations

- Takes advantage of others

- Is jealous and belittling of others

- Behaves in an arrogant or haughty manner

- Demands special treatment

- Has difficulty regulating emotions and behavior

- Is unable to cope with stress, adapt to change, or both

- Is sarcastic and bitter

- Avoids adult responsibilities by acting passive and helpless

- Intensely fears abandonment

- Has a pessimistic or negative life view

- Has difficulty being alone

- Shows disregard for right and wrong

- Persistently lies or deceives to exploit others

- Is callous, cynical, and disrespectful of others

- Uses charm or wit to manipulate others for personal gain or personal pleasure

- Is extremely opinionated

- Has recurring problems with the law, including criminal behavior

- Repeatedly violates the rights of others through intimidation and dishonesty

- Lacks empathy for others or remorse for harming others

- Fails to consider the negative consequences of behaviors or to learn from them

After reading through this list, I hope you feel validated in your own decision to establish no contact, or perhaps feel more courage to make this decision. The list validates that the abuse and manipulation you have experienced is real.

Flawed Versus Toxic Family Members

All people display toxic traits or behavior from time to time, as none of us is perfect. In this example I will focus specifically on parents, but this knowledge can also be applied to your other toxic family members. Any parent will inadvertently cause their children pain. Life is hard, and it is not possible for even the most healthy parents to be emotionally available in each moment their children need them. If you're a parent yourself, you are bound to have your own parenting moments you deeply regret. However, these normal lapses in parenting do not qualify you as toxic.

These less-than-stellar moments are human and normal. The difference is that, as a healthy parent, you feel terrible when you hurt your children. Your natural feelings of guilt and remorse motivate you to repair the damage. You do not take the shame you feel about yourself and justify it by casting blame onto your children.

But toxic family members do this. They find it easier on their fragile ego to view others as responsible for causing their bad moments. Toxic parents twist your innocent mind to believe that if you had just been better and/or needed less, they would have done better as parents. As a child you cannot fathom that your parents could ever be wrong. Children unknowingly absorb and identify with the shame wrongly cast on them for actions and conflicts they did not cause. Instead, in each shaming instance, as a child you learn to believe you are "bad."

What I, you, and many other survivors come to terms with over time is the harsh reality that our family members did not and do not genuinely love us. Not because there was anything wrong with us as their child, sibling, or cousin, but because they do not value love itself. What your toxic family members value is power.

In my case, my mother fake-loved me. I always felt she loved me because she had to. She loved me because I was an obligation. I know this to be true because I have always felt her disdain for me and seen her differential treatment of my other family members. I have certainly experienced moments of her intermittent doses of kindness and attention (which is necessary for manipulation to be effective) that kept me hooked into the belief that she loved me, but deep down I always *knew*. I could see it on her face, feel it in her body language, and hear it in her tone of voice. Your instincts signal you when someone genuinely loves you, and my mother did not give me that feeling.

> **Take a Moment for You:** Reflect on whether you ever felt truly loved by your family member or members. Examine what you felt inside when you did not feel loved by your family and how you internalized this.

I believe when you know, deep in your soul, that the love your family should have naturally given you was not and is not there, you need to make choices that help you protect yourself from their abuses.

> **Moment of Insight:** In cutting ties, we change, we heal, we get heathier; our toxic family members do not.

The hardest part of this? It is scary to make a decision when you do not know many others who have had to do the same thing. There is no model or protocol to follow and no results, positive or negative, for you to observe. So it is tremendously helpful, before making any life-changing decisions, to have an idea of how many other people may have had to do the same thing. For that we can turn to statistics.

How Common Is Cutting Family Ties?

There are many people whose family members are so destructive that there is no healthy way to tolerate the psychological abuse they must endure to stay in a relationship. A 2015 U.S. study reported more than 40 percent of individuals had experienced family estrangement at one point in their lives. And while estrangement often encompasses extended family, it is common in immediate families as well. It was also reported that 10 percent of mothers are currently estranged from at least one adult child.[1]

Shahida Arabi, author of *Healing Adult Children of Narcissistics*, did a study of seven hundred participants who self-reported having

- A narcissistic mother: 36 percent

- A narcissistic father: 22 percent

- Both parents toxic: 14 percent

- A parent who showed a persistent lack of empathy: 86 percent

- A parent who exhibited self-centeredness: 84 percent

- A parent with an extreme sense of entitlement: 76 percent

- A parent who showed excessive rage in response to perceived criticism or slight: 74 percent[2]

More than eight hundred individuals contributed to "Hidden Voices: Family Estrangement in Adulthood," a joint project of the Centre for Family Research at the University of Cambridge (U.K.) and the charitable organization Stand Alone (n.d.). Participants included parents estranged from their children and children estranged from their parents, casting light on generational estrangement from two different perspectives. The study reports that:

- Over 50 percent of adult children estranged from a parent say they were the ones to cut off the contact.

- Only 5 to 6 percent of parents report that they were the person who cut contact.

- Of adult children estranged from their parents, 79 percent could not foresee having a functional relationship with their mother.

- Of adult children estranged from their parents, 71 percent reported they could never again have a functional relationship with their father.[3]

When questioned about what they wanted from their parents, adult children said "they wanted relationships that were closer, more positive, and more loving. In addition, they wished their mothers would be less critical and judgmental, and that mothers would acknowledge when they have engaged in hurtful behavior. These same adult children wished their fathers would take more interest in their lives and also stand up to other family members, including their spouses or partners."[4]

Chances are you can identify with the thoughts and feelings of those interviewed for these studies. I hope your knowing that up to 40 percent of people have been estranged from family at some point will help substantiate the reasoning behind your own decision. You may wonder why you did not know that the statistics on cutting ties were as high as they are. Now imagine how high the statistics would be if all the people in your situation reported their abuse—well beyond 40 percent. Many don't report their .abuse because so many have been overtly or covertly manipulated to not share the family secrets.

The Silent Epidemic of Family Estrangement

The reason you know so little about what life is like being estranged from family is that many survivors choose to keep their suffering quiet. Thus it makes sense that, because family estrangement is seldom talked about, it is also widely misunderstood. Some survivors do not speak openly of the estrangement because they fear it may be humiliating. Others fear sounding cruel; still others prefer to keep family issues private to avoid unwanted shame or judgment.

The purpose of this book is to use my personal experience as a survivor of estrangement from my own family, and the personal experiences of many of my patients and social media followers, coupled with my knowledge as a leading expert in my field, to help those of you divided from family to live a life of deep meaning and purpose. I aim to bring the shame and confusion you feel out of the dark and into the light for conversation, examination, permission, validation, and healing. I know it is possible for you to pivot and transform what was intended to harm you into something amazing and deeply impactful.

To accomplish this, you must come to feel proud of the decisions you have made, or are in a position to make, regarding protections you have—or need to—set in place from family members who are deeply damaging to your mental health and well-being. Regardless of what you will face on the road ahead with your family, honor yourself for the decisions you have made that help keep you in charge of your own life.

Chapter 2

Why You Still Hurt

In the aftermath of cutting ties, you hurt. Not because you are necessarily looking for connection or conversation with your family, but because it is hard to imagine any family member—especially a parent, sibling, adult child, cousin, or grandparent—being okay with not seeing their own children, grandchildren, siblings, cousins, or parents. It's a surreal feeling to realize your toxic family members would rather never see you or your children again than to offer a simple apology after you have stood up to their abusive behavior. It is powerful enough to stop you in your tracks. This is when you realize they have no remorse. Digesting that can feel like swallowing sand.

I never could have foreseen or imagined how much there was to learn about the reality of life after cutting ties with my toxic family members. I have been learning—and want you to know—that it is normal to vacillate between the joy of newfound freedom and the doubt that comes along with the decision. This inner conflict is made vivid in the Disney movie *Tangled*, which I recommend watching. Put yourself in the shoes of the main character, Rapunzel, as she escapes Mother Gothel—who is like your family. To get her freedom, Rapunzel has to betray her mother so she can discover herself.

As Rapunzel escapes the tower prison of isolation that Mother Gothel forced upon her, she sails downward toward the ground that she was forbidden to touch. Right before she is about to reach it, Rapunzel pauses and experiences a moment of terror. Slowly and cautiously Rapunzel touches her toes to the grass to see if it is safe. Once she feels secure, she leaps into the grass and sings with elation. In shock, she exclaims, "I can't believe I did this" while jumping up and down, arms spread wide, looking out to the enormous expanse of this new life. She is seeing the world from a brand-new perspective: freedom, no barriers, no entrapment, no oppression.

Then, in one torturous moment, she stoops over, pulls her arms in close, and mutters with sheer horror about how her mother would react. She rocks back and forth as her fears overwhelm her. Still, soon Rapunzel is running, wildly yelling, "This is so much fun!" as she joyfully kicks a pile of leaves and sends them floating into the air. Her mood rapidly changes: she perches on a tree branch and whispers, *"I'm a horrible daughter; I'm going back."* Two seconds later she is tumbling and rolling down a hill, screaming with joy about how she's *never* going back. Soon after that, lying face down in complete despair, she decides she is a despicable human being. In the next swift second, she is swinging exuberantly by her hair, singing to all the land. But her excitement quickly ends. Defeated and crying into her hands, she feels the weight of the duplicity she is inflicting on Mother Gothel. The man she escaped with approaches her and observes that she seems to be at war with herself.

Rapunzel's shifting and conflicting emotions are exactly what the aftermath of cutting ties feels like. We are stuck between the exciting feelings of freedom and the horrible feelings of guilt and doubt at the thought of "betraying" our family and the system of emotional imprisonment they held us in. However, consider the irony. I encourage you to ask yourself this: *How can I betray what is abusive and already betraying me?* Can we betray betrayal? I think not. Neither did Rapunzel. Still, this confusion places us at war within ourselves throughout the aftermath of separating from family.

We can best understand this conflict as Stockholm syndrome, wherein the trapped person develops feelings of trust or affection toward their captor. For survivors of toxic family systems, these feelings are exacerbated by the fact that the people we are simultaneously affectionate toward and escaping from are the exact people we should be intimately attached to: our family.

Like Rapunzel, you'll find that your confidence will both increase and decrease after you free yourself from the poison of your family environment: first, because you are afraid deep down that perhaps you are the horrible, despicable person your family members claim you are; and second, because you may fear some type of karma-like punishment for "dishonoring" your family. And yet, like Rapunzel, you likely have never felt a stronger sense of your own internal power than after deciding to honor yourself by establishing definitive boundaries between yourself and your dysfunctional family.

My life and the lives of many of my patients and other survivors have only gotten increasingly better as time has passed, even though a host of new problems is unavoidable. You will discover that, just because you have estranged yourself from your psychologically abusive family members, it doesn't mean you no longer yearn to have a family—that is, a family as you would have wanted it to be.

Family should provide you with the sense of safety, security, and belonging you cannot fully replicate anywhere else or in any other relationship. These familial relationships are deeply fundamental to anyone's overall well-being. Moving away from the familiarity of family can leave you feeling exposed and unstable. Although your family environment was not a safe place, your family was still something fundamental, essential, and important that you belonged to. It is all you have ever known.

So be prepared for the aftermath to be filled with unknowns. It takes time to adjust to such a monumental change. It is normal that on some days you think about your family members a lot, and on other days they may not cross your mind at all. However, because you are bound to these people, be it biologically or adoptively, your relationship with them will remain active emotionally, mentally, and spiritually, even in a state of silence.

Moment of Insight: Sometimes you have to let go of what is killing you, even when it's killing you to let go.

The Quiet of the Aftermath

The best—though for some perhaps the worst—part of the aftermath is the quiet. It is a strange feeling to have silence in the space where the emotional noise of family should be. However, it makes sense when you understand that your family members do not view your silence to their abuse as an issue with them, but rather as a problem with you. They view your silence as a competition and often vow to out-silence you.

For me, the silence of the aftermath brought some relief. Like many survivors, I do not feel any desire to pick up the phone, nor do I consider seeing my family again. I have too much evidence of how my old "going back" pattern served only to set me up for further abuse. I have learned to love the space from my family and the feeling of protection gained from not being in contact. However, admittedly, on other days the silence has been and can still be lonely, shocking, and painful. If you feel these same ways, you are not alone.

Similar to you, me, and others, my patient Gina gets intensely triggered when her sister sends her daughter gifts for holidays and birthdays but will not acknowledge Gina on any of these occasions. On the face of it, this may seem hypocritical, since Gina chooses to have no contact with her sibling; however, when no-contact boundaries are established, those boundaries must also apply to the children of the person who has severed ties.

But toxic family members do not consider how they could work things out with you in a way that would, for example, make someone like Gina feel comfortable with her sister's establishing a healthy relationship with her niece. You should expect your toxic family members to avoid taking ownership, making any personal changes in their own behavior, or collaborating with you and your values. They turn the concept of love into a tit-for-tat game. They live from the idea of *If you cut me off, then I will cut you off, but I will still prey upon your children because they are my niece, nephew, or grandchild.* Unfortunately, competitive and exclusionary emotional games only increase your desire to enforce your no-contact boundaries with these family members even further.

Moment of Insight: Innocent family members? Not when they are toxic.

Take a Moment for You: Reflect on the idea that your toxic family members are people who willingly and intentionally participate in a system—be it work, play, or relationship—that is unhealthy for you and others. Knowing this is an important layer of your healing. The next step is understanding why your family members are like this.

Expect Strong Bonds to Haunt You

When it comes to accurately describing how it feels to remove yourself from your own family, words can seem inadequate. Feeling that you are easy to overlook or simply do not matter to the people you should matter to the most is terrifying and isolating. These feelings are deeply embedded in the beliefs you learn to hold about yourself as you grow up. Learning to cope with such tumultuous emotions is typical of growing as a person in the aftermath of cutting ties. The emotions and unhealthy attitudes you were raised to have about yourself can be difficult to change and overcome, but it can be done.

I do not know if there is science to back this up, but I believe there is something emotional about how genetics bond us. Even when you are happy with your decision to be in a protective place of no contact, you will still carry a part of you that mourns what you never had, what you should have had; a part that wonders whether *you* were—or are—the real problem. Parts of you will still be susceptible to your family members' manipulations and abuses, even after severing ties, because you are their child, sibling, niece, grandchild, or parent, regardless of your age, knowledge, or life experience. When you're at your lowest following trauma, it is only natural to turn to family for support. This natural desire to love your family and for them to love you in return is confusing. You may wonder, *If I still want their love and support, am I doing the right thing by severing ties?*

Moment of Insight: You gravitate toward the familiar because it gives you a false sense of security or safety. Most survivors will unconsciously choose familiar pain over an unknown alternative.

It's hard to feel completely comfortable with the decision to sever ties with your family. Feelings of doubt will plague you on and off throughout the process. This kind of confusion is healthy and normal because you are a naturally caring and loving person. This isn't one of those decisions you can be completely sure about before making it. But I hope you won't allow this to hold you back from making a decision that will set you free from the abuse and manipulation you have been suffering.

Confidence Is Not Needed

I was once asked in an interview what skills I could offer to help others develop the confidence to cut ties with their toxic family members. I let the interviewer know I did not sever ties from a place that felt anything like skill or confidence. Like many survivors, I cut ties because the continued psychological damage inflicted by my family was so unlivable, I had no other healthy choice. I explained that the decision had grown, morphed, and developed over forty-five years of trying every failed way to stay connected to my family. In the end, the decision came down to two options: to stay in a burning building, or jump. I finally chose to jump for the chance of creating a happier and healthier life for myself. The lies, betrayals, and cruelties thrown at me throughout my life were so vile and calculated, I knew my only reasonable choice was to protect myself. I did not *want* to sever ties; I *had* to. It was a decision not of confidence, but of survival.

When you sever ties, it's only natural to lack confidence: you have no proof or basis of experience to know whether your decision is going to work in your favor or make your life even worse. The self-doubt this brings can make you mercilessly question yourself. You start searching for certainty in a situation where there can be none. That's why it can help to revisit the running list (in chapter 1) of toxic traits that have long sabotaged your reaching this decision. The list will remind you of the accumulated damage you've endured at the hands of your family. You can trust this list, and it will prove to be a helpful aid for the remainder of your life.

Caught in a Mental Loop

Sharon described her thoughts about her family as existing in a never-ending loop. In this loop her thoughts and feelings swirl around in the confusion of the whys and hows that can explain her family members' being the way they are. But her search for answers will not resolve her pain.

When the answers bring no relief, Sharon boils over with emotion as she questions what she did, past and present, that was so wrong or so bad to her parents and siblings. As Sharon mutters these thoughts out loud, she usually launches into the list of all the good things she has done for her family. She then repeats the list of the deplorable damage done to herself by her parents and siblings. Two of her three siblings have taken their own lives. As much as this reality helps her understand that she is not the problem, she still lives with this undefined lingering doubt about herself and her own personal value.

Like Sharon, you may be asking these kinds of unanswerable questions:

- Why didn't my parents or siblings care?

- Why didn't my extended family members step in to help?

- Why didn't any effort send a strong enough message to my family that maybe they needed to look in the mirror?

- Why wasn't I, the supposed love of a parent's life, worth this sacrifice?

This type of endless mental loop is familiar to those with abusive family dynamics. It is easy to see why it is so hard for you to understand the reasons your family members do not love you enough to say they're sorry, genuinely mean it, and make the appropriate changes in their behavior that a normal healthy person would make to repair the relationship.

How can our beloved family members be so callous?

The answer is painful: They do not care.

Is this simply not caring truly possible?

The answer, again, is painful: Yes, it is.

We need to understand that this inability to show empathy or concern for another, especially one of their own blood, is the critical difference between an ordinary flawed person and one who is toxic.

Abusers do have good moments. They have days where they do and say the right things. Unfortunately, all this accomplishes is to confuse you and give you false hope.

> **Moment of Insight:** An abuser having a good day does not take away from the fact that they are still an abuser.

You are staying away from your family because you understand what family means to you, and the meaning you hold does not include abuse or manipulation of any kind. Therefore, you must vow to yourself that you will never again be forced or coerced into being mistreated by the family members who were supposed to love and protect you the most fiercely.

Coping with Self-Doubt

When you are severing ties, it is okay to struggle with questioning and doubting yourself. It is all part of the healing process. It's not possible to rid yourself of the primal human need for a supportive, loving family. Further, even when you fully separate yourself from your abusers and feel content with your decision, you will naturally still have a feeling of emptiness. It makes sense that you would feel empty of love, of having a trusted tribe. You feel empty of security, kindness, compassion, trust, stability, and safety—all the things that healthy family members would provide.

Sadly, on an unconscious level, no matter how sure you are of your decision to set yourself free, you may still crave permission to do what you have done—or at least some kind of verbalized acceptance of your decision to sever ties—from your family members themselves. Yet you have enough experience to know it is a fantasy to think your family members would ever say, "We have treated you horribly, and it is understandable you would feel the need to separate from us to have a chance at feeling and experiencing the happiness and love you deserve," and to give you that closure you long for. This longing points to the need for boundaries—to help you draw a line not only between yourself and your toxic family members, but also between those old longings and expectations, and the life you are going to pursue as you leave them behind.

Chapter 3

See Boundaries as Good to Have

Personal boundaries are simple guidelines, rules, or limits you create to establish reasonable, safe, and unfettered ways for others to behave when relating to you. They include how you will respond when or if someone violates those limits. Unfortunately, when it comes to setting boundaries, it seems we are given permission to do this with anyone and everyone *except* our family. How does this make sense? Why would persons defined as "family" be excused?

Our larger society gives the message that you are cruel to set boundaries on those who raised you or on those whom you were raised with, especially when you set these boundaries on family as an adult. This message contributes to your own unhealthy pattern of not looking to see where the responsibility may lie with the other players involved in your current life when something goes wrong. Instead, you may reflexively, critically, and mercilessly examine yourself for fault. It may not occur to you that maybe someone else holds some level of culpability because you were not raised to have any boundaries.

But solid boundaries will help you to cut ties and then maintain the distance. Physical boundaries let the good things in and keep the bad things out. Emotional boundaries are not as obvious to the naked eye but are equally important, especially with family, where emotional boundaries are blurred if you don't make them clear. Emotional boundaries involve separating your feelings from another's.

Moment of Insight: Boundaries are a statement of your self-respect.

Your family members will likely feel slighted about boundaries you apply to them. That is not your problem. That is about the stuff they will need to clean up in their life (or not). You do not need to let them violate boundaries by taking upon yourself responsibility for their feelings, letting their feelings dictate your own, sacrificing your own needs in order to please them, allowing them to blame you for their problems, or accepting responsibility for their problems. How do you know where your boundaries need to be? By listening to your pain. When you feel hurt, you must examine what you will and will not tolerate.

You do not cut ties with family because you are coldhearted, unfeeling, or lacking in kindness. In fact, it is just the opposite. You establish limits because you hold concern and protection for your own wounds, and you care to safeguard others.

Setting boundaries with your abusive family members opens your choices and options to heal and succeed in the ways you desire. When you are not being poisoned by your family, you are allowed to be happy, to be yourself, to say no, to state your opinions, to love who you want, do what you want, and say what needs to be said—and to do all of this freely. This is how life should have always been for you.

> **Moment of Insight:** You set boundaries because you care about values like fairness and the meaning of genuine love.

It can be difficult to find support from others when it comes to your severing ties with your family, because many people cannot understand your need to do this. But you do not have to obtain other people's understanding to feel the permission you would like to feel to do what is best for you.

Let Go of the Need for Permission

The surest step you take in changing your life is always the hardest. This step comes when you set the first boundary of severing ties with your family because you recognize that you cannot heal in the same environment that is poisoning you. Cutting ties is no joke. It takes a tremendous amount of courage. It is a hard and painful process to endure, because when you remove yourself from your family you want to feel, no matter your age, that you *do* have the permission and support necessary to do this.

But it is unfortunate how many people in our culture refuse to grant this permission. According to Cloud and Townsend, in their book *Boundaries*, there are valid reasons you need this support from those closest to you to set and maintain your boundaries:

- One of your primal needs is for love and belonging. People will suffer tremendously in order to have and keep relationships.

- The fear of being alone keeps many of us tied to our dysfunctional family for years. There is little to no support for those considering taking this step—not from churches, from most therapists, or even from friends. The lack of support only makes you more afraid to set and maintain the boundaries that can free you, because you erroneously (but understandably) assume that if you were doing something right, others would have no problem supporting you.

- You need support to dispel the fear that if you set correct and healthy boundaries with your family, this will lead to your no longer having love in your life.[5]

Setting definitive boundaries will inadvertently place you in a double bind: You will not be granted permission to take this action by your destructive family, and you will likely not find a lot of support from those who believe there is good in all people. Instead, you end up battling against other people's desires to fix your problem for you so *they* can feel comfortable with *your* family dynamic. This raises the question: Why does anyone else need to feel comfortable with your family dynamic? Because of their own personal discomfort with something that is not fitting nicely into a box? In fact, some people will likely offer to help you reestablish their vision of peace between yourself and your family members, not so *you* can be comfortable, but so *they* can be. You do not need approval or permission from others to establish the necessary boundaries to protect yourself. The only permission you need comes from the feelings inside you telling you that you need to make yourself safe.

I encourage you to listen more strongly to yourself than to others when it comes to your own experience. It is a hard but valiant practice to let go of your need for permission to establish the boundaries you know you need. The permission you give yourself is more than enough, because it is your life to live—not anyone else's.

> **Moment of Insight:** The strength of your boundaries can be stronger than your doubt.

Your family will not like having boundaries set on them. They feel entitled to get their way when it comes to the relationship *they have with you* because they do not consider what kind of relationship *you have with them*. But it is time to decide, for yourself, what you will and will not tolerate in your life.

Identify Lines of Tolerance

The greatest gift that boundaries offer is the distinguishing line between where another person stops and you start. It is at the firm separation between yourself and the other that your instincts alert you to when something sacred in your personal/emotional space has been inappropriately violated. Setting a boundary to protect that sacred space helps you avoid further hurt and/or misunderstanding at this line. If you have destructive relationships consuming your space, you are taking responsibility for the wrong things and people. However, boundaries are not rigidly black and white. Boundaries must leave room for flexibility, within reason. Here are some tips for assessing degrees of tolerance to use when setting boundaries:

- *Define your limits:* You must decide what you will or will not tolerate.

- *Pay attention to feelings of resentment:* Such feelings let you know when someone has been forcefully imposing their personal expectations, views, demands, or values on you without your consent or interest.

- *Be direct or be silent:* There are two ways to set boundaries. First, be direct with the person or people crossing your boundaries by telling them how you feel when they engage in the behaviors that create your discomfort. This method works best in relationships that are mutually reciprocal and open to feedback. With toxic people, the second method—silence—is nearly always most effective, because a toxic person will hold everything you do and say against you.

- *You have rights:* Fear and guilt are the greatest pitfalls when it comes to established lines of tolerance. You are an adult, and until you start standing up for what is right, you cannot secure full ownership over your life or its direction.

- *Honor your feelings:* The more you listen to your feelings and the more self-awareness you develop, the better you position yourself to set the correct boundaries that enable you to take proper care of your life.

- *Seek advice:* If it is too hard to tell whether you are being overly sensitive to something someone has said or done, or if you fear you may be misunderstanding something, seek advice before setting boundaries you may later regret.

- *Be patient:* Setting boundaries is both an art and a science. Boundaries need to be strategic, in that you communicate clearly with your family members what your needs and limits are, while also tailoring your communication to get the least amount of kickback. As you begin this journey, it is a good practice to start with setting small boundaries; for example, "Unfortunately, this week is busy and I cannot talk." As you gain small successes, you'll develop the confidence to start setting the larger, more significant limits, such as, "When you treat me poorly, I will remove myself from your presence."

If you allow your life to be unprotected, you live feeling paranoid, isolated, and scared, a tragically smaller version of the person you are meant to be. Boundaries give you the emotional muscle necessary to live a full life. If you feel it is wrong to have to—or want to—set limits, you must work to overcome that feeling.

> **Moment of Insight:** Problems that come into your life from others are not your problem.

Dos and Don'ts After Severing Ties

Once you have severed ties, *do* take care of yourself at all costs. Do *not* answer calls, emails, or letters, or respond to gifts, cards, or other forms of contact initiated by your family. In any type of emergency, you will likely be contacted by someone your family uses to reach out to you (we'll discuss this topic in further detail shortly). *Do* take those calls while letting the person who contacts you know about your boundaries around your family. *Do* thank these people for their concern, and for the information they have given you. Nothing more. *Do* remember that the most important job you have is taking care of yourself, and the only ones you need to be loyal to, post cutting ties, are you and those closest to you.

The Double Bind of Twisted Nonsense

Things get complicated when you try to explain to others why you feel you had no other choice. This is when you must dig deep and trust that you have made the correct decision for yourself, even as others project onto you their often nonsensical reasons why you have made the absolute wrong decision.

It is not possible for anyone to fix your family dysfunction for you, but nonetheless, in the aftermath of cutting ties you often face those who have little experience with toxicity but will nevertheless try to fix things. When you hold firm to the lines you have drawn, this often aggravates the fixers. In their aggravation, they erroneously view *you* as the stubborn and unforgiving person, and the circle of projection begins to spin. They ignorantly believe that if you would reconnect with your family, your abuse would stop. And where does that put you? Back to square one.

This irrational loop of twisted nonsense is sure to challenge your emotions and your sanity. These fixers do not think deeply enough to consider that, if you have reached a decision as serious as cutting ties, you have already done the work, been through the pain, and asked all the pertinent questions. I often ponder the paradox of why, when no-contact boundaries are established between a child and a parent, or any younger person and an older family member, the younger person is seen as the unreasonable party in the dynamic; yet when parents or older family members set boundaries based on the lack of respect they receive from their adult child or younger family member, such as a niece or grandchild, they are viewed as good parents and aunts, uncles, or grandparents. This makes no sense.

In the aftermath, you may battle this type of blind hypocrisy when it comes to general ideas or definitions of "family" and how family dynamics should be. You'll need to examine this hypocrisy so you can work through the confusion when you face the hypocrites and continue, without wavering, to hold tightly to the truth of your own experience.

> **Take a Moment for You:** Reflect on the hypocrisy in your own family. Write down all the rules that they rigidly apply to you but do not follow themselves. Describe how this negatively impacts you—for example, by making the relationship a one-way experience, not directed in your favor.

Opening Canned Perceptions of Family

The canned perceptions around family that society generally holds can wreak havoc on those who set the necessary boundaries with their abusers. Viewed from a place of understanding, we can see that it is hard for others to support your decision because they do not want to be perceived, or to perceive themselves, as persons who do not value family. Because so many are leery of this topic, it creates a seemingly endless uphill battle for survivors to feel understood. Your willingness to confront this battle and stand firm in the face of such a blatant lack of acceptance speaks to just how toxic your family environment must have been if you prefer this type of scrutiny to staying attached to your family. Yet, for whatever reason, the message still does not seem clear to others. That is just how difficult the value of family is to penetrate and why so many remain prisoners to the control and exploitations of predatory family members.

Bottom line: behaviors have consequences. Whatever a person puts into the world will have an equal consequence. Cloud and Townsend, in *Boundaries*,[6] teach that when your family members ignore the law of sowing and reaping, there are consequences. The law of cause and effect asserts that severe consequences await anyone who does intentional harm to another. If you choose to rescue or protect people from the natural consequences their behavior merits, you render them powerless. Family members who emotionally abuse and manipulate you position themselves to face the natural consequences that match their behavior. What is the natural consequence of their poor treatment? The loss of the relationship.

Families who love and respect each other, who provide healthy limits with warmth and consequence, are families that get along in a loving and mutually respectful manner, with each member able to embrace their individual differences from others in a spirit of openness and acceptance. This is not the type of environment you were raised in. Therefore you should not feel guilty for giving your psychologically abusive family members the natural consequences of their behavior. If you spare them these consequences, they have no opportunity to learn from them.

Dropping Family Titles as a Boundary

One of the most powerful boundaries I set, which I believe may also be helpful and healing for you, was coming to an understanding that, for me as an adult, my toxic family members are just people; they are not authorities. When you are a child, parents or older family members (siblings, aunts, uncles, grandparents, cousins) always have the most power in the relationship. They are your everything, but not necessarily because they have earned it. They are bigger, older, and capable of independent living. You are to follow their lead and do as they tell you. You model them; you seek their love, approval, support, guidance, time, love, and attention. You are to be quiet and not complain. You are not to question or go against them. Whatever they say goes. You do all you can to display the correct behaviors that will meet their expectations to make them happy and proud of you.

However, these rules apply only if you are living under their roof. I will never forget the day I no longer considered my sibling, mother, or father to be my family. After enough time tolerating their abuse, and one pinnacle event that showcased the depth of their cruelty, it was clear that the only thing they would ever be to me were people, *just people*. When you give people titles such as "mother," "father," "sister," "brother," and so on, you give them importance, leadership, and power in your life. When you were born, they had those titles, and you had no choice but to honor them. Once you attain adulthood, you may not be able to legally divorce your family, but you can divorce them emotionally. When I was forced to accept, in one moment as an adult, just how evil my family members could be, I stopped calling them by family title names. I have been calling them by their given names ever since. This has done wonders for me and for many of my patients, psychologically. I want the same for you.

> **Moment of Insight:** When your family members don't deserve the power a familial title bestows, take it away from them.

This simple boundary will remind you that your family members are just ordinary people. It will help you accept them for exactly who they are. If they no longer have familial, leadership, or relationship roles in your life, it is appropriate for you to no longer give them the titles and positions they once had that their abuse and manipulation destroyed. As the wise Dumbledore said in the *Harry Potter* series, "Call him Voldemort, Harry. Always use the proper name for things. Fear of a name increases the fear of the thing itself."

New Ways up the Mountain

Most people in tough emotional situations tend to choose the path of avoidance rather than a path of taking bold action. I did this for years with my family. I suggest we challenge our desire to avoid conflict and find new ways up the mountain so we can reach a more beautiful summit with vast views of fresh possibilities. If you really want to experience this summit, you must ask yourself: *Will avoidance of setting myself free from abusive relationships help me get there?* It will not. At some point, to be healthy and happy, you must do what is right for your overall well-being.

You do not have to avoid reality and end up living your life as a hopelessly timid pleaser, afraid of conflict. This fear keeps you tied to the people and circumstances that have been destroying you. It does take tremendous bravery to challenge the status quo. It also takes a tremendous amount of self-regard to do so, especially when going against the rigidly held belief that "family is everything." Family may indeed be everything for *some,* just not for *all.* The latter group deserves as much validation for our decision to leave abusive family as others deserve for honoring and staying connected to their healthy family.

Moment of Insight: People are entitled to their opinion about you and the actions you take, but they are not entitled to tell you what your decisions should be or what actions you should or should not take. That is solely up to you.

Take a Moment for You: Reflect on the power you would feel if you no longer made yourself a slave to what other people thought of you. List which actions to protect yourself would increase your feelings of empowerment.

You will need this empowerment. In destructive family systems, conflict is handled with the behavioral paradigm of "an eye for an eye and a tooth for a tooth." Therefore, when something bad happens, your family will seek revenge. Most often, the initial ties to the relationship between yourself and your family are cut by your toxic family when they discard you for not acquiescing to their abuses or manipulations. The ties stay cut only when you stand up for yourself and make the self-respecting decision that it is no longer your responsibility to repair damage not caused by you, and you then choose to stay silent. Your silence *does* offer your family members the choice and room to repair the relationship, but psychologically abusive people prefer revenge over repair. I'll describe how to handle their efforts in later chapters. For now, feel how worthy this boundary work is, for it gets you to a point where it no longer matters whether people believe and understand you; where all that matters is your courage and psychological wherewithal, and the actions you continue to take, to protect yourself against the predatory people in your life.

Chapter 4

The Critical Need to Grieve

When you have been placed in the position of setting healthy, definitive boundaries on the abuses and manipulations of toxic family members, you can expect tremendous emotional pain. It is more challenging than most could ever imagine, and it is a horribly sad position to be placed in. Your sadness and grief are justified.

You are losing something that seems deeply essential to the basic functioning of your life. You will rarely meet any person who would have willingly chosen the path you have been forced onto, of having to cut ties with your own blood to protect your psychological health and safety. But you now know that in setting the correct boundaries, you are also opening your life up to greater possibilities for happiness.

Unfortunately, many will not understand, and few will have empathy for you or your grief. Some will naively blame you for causing your own pain, since it was your decision to cut ties when, according to them, you didn't have to. This projection from others is based in ignorance: they have no idea what you have lived through for your entire life.

When you feel you are not supported or allowed to grieve, your feelings of resentment and rejection stay rooted inside your body, eroding your overall health and well-being. When you are not given permission to feel sad about your circumstances and to mourn them, you become deeply pained and internally isolated. The pain that others cannot see from the outside is that, in a healthy family paradigm, conflicts are handled with more benevolence, civility, and maturity. When something bad happens, healthy family members first reach for feelings. They reach for grieving. They reach for connection. They reach for understanding. They reach for compassion. They do not reach for revenge. Instead, they remain curious about what is needed to find an open and safe common ground. This did not and likely will not happen for you; therefore, you have the right to grieve and mourn the pain of the reality your family brings.

Moment of Insight: Grieving is what starts your healing.

It isn't until you have your family members secured behind protective boundaries that your grief work can truly begin. The beauty of cutting ties is you can finally start to discover who you really are when not under the negative influence of your conflict-obsessed family members. I suggest you put intention into your grieving. Focus your intention on establishing a loving and positive connection within yourself.

You Have a Right to Your Feelings

Your parents or other family members did not love you as you needed and deserved to be loved; you have every right to process and mourn this. You have the right to be angry and frustrated with your family for lying to you and grossly understating your value as an important and vital person in their life and in this world.

When your needs to express feeling sad, angry, and broken were met with canned, critical, indifferent, or dishonest responses, you were not being protected, loved, or given any real guidance from the people who were supposed to be your leaders and comrades. Instead, you were most often left feeling confused, worthless, frustrated, and without clear answers on how to approach them with your honest feelings and thoughts. It is nearly impossible not to become lost to yourself under the following types of abuse:

- You were overly criticized and emotionally damaged in your own home, and your valid grievances about your abuse have been thrown out by your family members, among others, as "completely crazy." This has led you to suffer from deep levels of self-doubt, confusion, shame, and self-hate.

- Sadly, in families such as yours, you learn to push your grief aside by punishing yourself for thinking such "horrible" (but valid) thoughts about your family.

- Growing up, you did not have the opportunity to connect, or be sad, with others. Nor were you allowed to feel your sadness privately. Your family provided no sense of community and no soft place to fall when you needed it most.

- No apologies were given, nor were there reciprocal efforts to work things out. Your feelings of being outcast and unloved were not repaired.

You need to understand that it is nearly impossible for anyone to maintain their sanity, let alone a realistic viewpoint of who they are, under the pressure of having to suppress every horrible feeling in order to keep their family happy. You need and deserve to feel all you must so that you can heal.

Steps to Healthy Grieving

Here are some practical steps to help guide you through your grief:

1. *Acknowledge and grieve the abusive and dismissive ways in which your family has mishandled your humanity.* List the misdeeds done to you, and acknowledge where you didn't get the validation or compassion you sought and deserved just out of basic human decency. One of the greatest ways to bring these memories up is to write to a F*ck You For list. I do this often with my patients. Begin each sentence with F*ck You For, and complete the sentence with the painful, angering, or frustrating memory. This exercise helps move you from feeling like a victim to taking the trash out. It places accountability on the right people. It also illuminates areas of growth for you, as you may feel anger at yourself for how long you allowed yourself to be passive or submissive to the members of your family you felt had power over you.

2. *Stop chasing, convincing, grasping, defending, explaining, and clutching abusive relationships for fear of not belonging.* The need to be vindicated is powerful in all of us. However, we must closely manage this need. It can be strong enough to keep you convinced that if you keep pursuing your family with your truth about their abusive treatment, they will eventually come around and give you the validation you seek. They won't. They will argue it, deny it, flip the script, and call you crazy. So how do you let go? You unhook from that compulsion for vindication. When you feel that compulsion energy rising up, recognize it and redirect it. Go outside and garden, go on a hike, go for a run, take notes about your urges and tell your therapist or a trusted friend, or let it go through prayer or giving it up to the universe. When you find yourself obsessing over the injustices of your family, bring your thoughts, your energy, and your focus back to yourself and your own life.

3. *Change your view that losing a relationship means you are not enough.* This is a self-talk exercise. Remind yourself that just because someone is a family member does not mean they abide by any sense of truth or integrity; that perhaps their need to treat you poorly is more a reflection of their dysfunction than anything to do with your worth. When you remind yourself of this truth often enough, it will become a truth you can count on.

4. *Get to know your hurt and humiliation; sit with your self-doubt and understand your inner critic.* You cannot skip over your emotions. Many of us often wish we could. Human emotions, by their very nature, are "passing through" energies—they come and they go. When your emotions come, you can train yourself to feel them without acting on them. When you discipline yourself to do this, you develop mastery over your emotions. Not every emotion you feel needs to be expressed. When you react out of raw emotion, you gain nothing productive; most often you're left feeling ashamed and powerless. Instead, take a slower, deeper approach to getting to know yourself. When you have gained self-control, it renders your toxic family members powerless to further harm you.

5. *Cry, sob, grieve, flail, scream, ache, and hold yourself close.* This may seem to contradict the preceding advice, but when your heart is truly breaking, it *can* be helpful to let all your feelings out—privately. Embrace the ugly cry, curse the gods, rage, tantrum, sob, feel your fear, and ache all over. This is healthy. Grief is designed to release pent-up negative, nonproductive energy. If you feel stuck behind defensive walls that block your ability to grieve, there are ways to bring down those walls. For example, you can rent a Rage Room. Here you use whatever is provided to beat the crap out of padded walls, heavy bags, and the like. Another way to unleash your grief is to write letters you do not send, or have imaginary conversations with the family members who have hurt you. Whatever form of pure abandon you choose, I guarantee you positive transformation. Most important, when you embrace your grief you get the honor of being the support for yourself that you have always sought from the family you thought you needed.

6. *Identify and eliminate voices born not of your own choice but of your family's manipulative programming.* The negative tapes of mistruths you have heard about yourself that keep playing in your mind will lose their power as you go through your grieving process. Consider the negative messages about you held by your family; practice replacing those lies with more accurate, positive testaments to the person you and many others know you are. When you feel insecure or unsure, these positive, more accurate statements will pull you back to your power.

7. *Give yourself the proper time, love, and attention required to listen to the pain that drives your grief.* It's natural to want to rush through the grieving process, because grieving hurts. But anything rushed is often incomplete, so you return to your grief over and over. If you're sad, angry, disgusted, and frustrated, let it be. Feel it. Intense feelings will come and they will go—if only you allow them to come. Take your time, open your heart, listen to what your emotions tell you, grab the lesson, and allow the emotions to pass through.

8. *Work to change the defeatist narrative of yourself that you learned to hold.* Negative, fatalistic thinking patterns driven by fear, paranoia, and anxiety are par for the course coming from a toxic family system. To shift your negative, fear-based narrative, start talking kindly and patiently with yourself. Take a minute to imagine the worst-case scenario happening, based on your fears. Give it as much detail as possible. Next, imagine your best-case scenario, with similar detail. As you allow your imagined worst-case scenario to play out, you will find it losing its power. It is emotionally driven, and…emotions come and then they go. The more aware you become that your worst-case scenario isn't rational, the more you'll refine your best-case scenario and the actions needed to make it your reality.

9. *Love yourself as if you were your own child.* The most important part of grieving is to generously give yourself the same compassion you would your own child or pet. Love yourself wholly. Be kind and patient with yourself. Encourage yourself. Respect yourself and the process of healing you're undertaking. Give yourself the time, love, rest, and attention you need, want, and deserve.

As you go through—and *grow* through—your grieving process, which is a lifelong venture, you start to see that there is light peeking through the clouds of despair you thought would never lift. In time you will start feeling hopeful rather than hopeless. When things start feeling hopeful, they naturally give your life a more positive cast.

Let's next consider the wonderful things you can look forward to as you journey through your mourning process.

> **Moment of Insight:** Grieving sets your soul right, cleanses your emotional palate, and gives you a new perspective on yourself, life, and relationships.

Grieving Allows You to Move On

Grieving is a continual and necessary process for you to undertake to move on from the family that has caused you so much heartache and pain. Grief helps you accept that it's not possible to find a healthy closure to every relationship, but this does not mean you cannot create closure for yourself. Closure comes not from the action of cutting ties, but when *you* decide the relationship is closed. Once you are firm in your decision, you can allow your family's abuses and manipulations to push you into a state of radical acceptance of your new reality. This acceptance means no admittance of your destructive family members and their poisonous influence into your life. And it opens you up to the many positive effects that can follow grieving:

- You start to live in the land of possibility, knowing that you are free from the oppression of the family that held you back.

- You start to notice that wonderful things are always happening to you and for you, and you start feeling a sense of fulfillment and satisfaction from life and relationships.

- You know how to manage your boundaries, and you no longer need to blame others when things do not go your way, because you have freed yourself from relationships that no longer serve you.

- You begin living in your own brave, humble, yet powerful radiance every single day.

- You are turned on by life rather than turned off.

- You find and develop a strong community of people who support and love you in the ways you have always desired, because you have learned to love yourself in all the ways fundamental to your living an abundant life.

- You can realize that life is a gift.

Grieving brings home the understanding that some people never apologize for the harm they have caused, because they simply will not. It is not that they *cannot* apologize; they simply *will not*. Although this may be difficult to accept, your family members will show themselves unable to move beyond their pride, to have the emotional intelligence to do what's necessary to repair the relationship with you. They view having to apologize as humiliating. They view apologizing as an act of defeat rather than a reparative win.

Moment of Insight: When you genuinely have a pure heart, no matter how big the hole in your heart may feel, you're sure to win in the end.

Grieving your family is essential. As you continue to educate yourself and allow yourself to mourn your losses, your grieving process will make you more resilient. Loss of family does leave a void in your heart, and that void will sometimes be triggered, especially in your social world. Remain open to continually feeling, grieving, and healing this void.

Along the way, as you come to deeper levels of helpful awareness, you'll learn that you cannot change emotionally immature family members, no matter how much you may think they need to change. This understanding sets you free to move on and focus on taking care of your own life. With your budding self-awareness, boundaries in place, and the desire to move forward, you can continue the journey of loving and taking care of yourself in ways that allow you to attract the healthy connections you have always desired to share in and experience.

You deserve to have these healthy connections; no one is built to thrive in a social void. Yet that is what the separation from family—however necessary—will create. We'll address this void in the next chapter.

Chapter 5

The Social Void of Broken Family Bonds

I hope that as you read you realize the void you have inside does not heal just because you have protected yourself from your family members with definitive boundaries. Those family members who were supposed to fill that void are still gone. And now, with no-contact boundaries, even more permanently. This brings both freedom and loss. Even as you grieve and work on healing and understanding your pain, this isn't shared work. It is solitary. You do grief work to fill the gaping void in your heart, the painful feelings of not belonging or fitting in with your family as you deserved to. When you establish no contact, you decrease their abuse but also deepen the hole in your life. Grief work helps you accept this dual and conflictual reality for what it is, even when this acceptance is forever heartbreaking on some level.

> **Moment of Insight:** The loss of family leaves a profound feeling of emptiness in your life.

To illustrate this void, we can use the 9/11 destruction of the Twin Towers of the World Trade Center as a metaphor. You should have had, as a birthright, two strong, indestructible, stable towers as parents, giving you and the entire family the safety, security, and fairness promised by their role as parents. But they didn't; they were a source of chaos, drama, and pain that collapsed the family system.

Where the towers stood, there are now memorial fountains. And extending the metaphor again, after years of your being manipulated, continually cast out, and returning only to be emotionally annihilated again and again, you, I, and many others finally reach a point where we prefer the calming sound of the cool running waters of the empty void to the inferno inside the family system.

When I went to visit the 9/11 memorial, I noticed that as people gaze down into the void-like fountains that honor the deceased, nearly everyone also looks upward, as if to affirm that those massive and amazing towers are *really truly* no longer there. The collapse of those remarkable towers is still so unbelievable that it is still, years and years later, beyond human comprehension. The same is true for the lost innocence of all children who deserved and needed two strong, remarkable, steady, indestructible, loving parents and other family members to support them throughout their life.

> **Take a Moment for You:** Reflect on the void in your life, and take note of how that feels personally, socially, and emotionally.

When your family system is poisoned with gossip, manipulation, and the pitting of siblings, parents, and other family members against each other, it will inevitably implode and come crashing down at some point. What may appear to others from the outside to be functional and indestructible may be too weak to hold things together forever. When a dysfunctional family system finally implodes, you are left quite naked and exposed in the social world in a way that is, unfortunately, noticeable to others. One challenge that can keep you from experiencing a sense of peace and confidence in the rightness of your decision to sever ties is the unwanted social and interpersonal intrusions that may present themselves for the remainder of your life, in one way or another. It seems that you trade one type of intrusiveness for another, as people naturally intrude on what is not, at first glance, clearly understandable to them interpersonally or socially.

To help you navigate some of these issues when they arise, I will describe what I and others have encountered. Learning to prepare for and cope with these intrusions will be integral to your healing.

Moment of Insight: Those who have separated from a toxic family are often treated like the addict who gets sober, with others questioning their sobriety for the remainder of their life. It is hard to ever feel trusted or understood.

Being Misunderstood by Others

Creating your freedom comes at a cost, because it's rare to meet others who are open about their own destructive family members, and most people can't understand why anyone would prefer zero or little connection with their family. When a stranger first meets you, and you appear relatively healthy, normal, and successful, they initially assume you must have come from a solid, loving, and supportive family. It shocks people when their assumption is vastly different from your reality.

When you share your experience, most people will share some type of personal story of their own to reason with you about why you should still have at least *one* tie to your family. They'll usually advise you to stay in contact with your family so you will have nothing to "regret" later in life. Their advice indicates they believe you are doing something fundamentally wrong in creating definitive boundaries. These advice-givers often include therapists who may have researched or studied toxic people but have no real firsthand life experience surviving in the depths of that type of trauma. It is not the psychological experts or researchers who know the most about what you go through. If you want to know how to survive the psychological stress—and the permanent void—of separating from a toxic family system, it's more helpful to listen to the stories of fellow survivors who have already suffered, then follow their lead.

Moment of Insight: The people with the greatest depth of knowledge about your experience are the fellow survivors.

The lack of understanding you encounter in your social network, no matter how innocent, becomes an unwanted invasion that often reawakens the pain of your family wound. This makes your situation not only painful but also frustrating, and your grief even more profound. Whenever you are given unsolicited feedback on your decision to cut ties, I give you permission to ignore any of the following projections:

- "Your family members do not mean to do what they do."

- "Your family members simply are not aware of the pain they cause."

- "You should just forgive and forget."

- "You must not be understanding your family members or their behavior correctly."

- "You are just being too sensitive."

With these erroneous assumptions and platitudes, people overtly dismiss the truth and depth of your pain. They fail to understand that their devil's advocate approach—trying to make you rethink your carefully considered, sound decisions—is little different from your experience of being gaslighted by your family whenever *they* disagreed with your decisions. This insensitive, intrusive approach can leave you feeling as if no one understands you and your unique situation, which is incredibly isolating.

Take a Moment for You: Do you trust your own perception, or do others pull you away from it? Write your response, and reflect on the fact that no one knows or understands your abusers better than you do. You do not have to explain or defend the hidden abuses you have undergone to anyone for any reason.

Unfortunately, when your pain is treated flippantly by others, you're naturally pulled toward being more reclusive. It is natural to question the point of sharing anything about your situation with anyone if you are just going to be met with misunderstanding. Why share, just so you can hear them give you examples from their own life that have no real relevance to the situation you left? This undoubtedly makes it difficult to trust people and to want to get close to them.

Social judgments can block deeper intimacy. When people are set against understanding and empathizing with your story, it disrupts the peace you are trying to establish in your life. Therefore you have the right to consider whether these people are right for you. In my life and in my patients' lives, I've observed that once you start cutting family out of your life, you recognize with more accuracy how many others, family or nonfamily, are not adding to your life but taking from it. This can be scary; it can seem as if your relationship world is going through a cleanse and there's nothing you can do to salvage some of it. You may worry whether there will be anyone left on your side at the end. These feelings are normal and understandable, because the end of other relationships is common after cutting ties with family.

Regardless of the detail and evidence you provide of what you have suffered, what you share may not illuminate enough clarity for the other's to understand and empathize with you. So you again feel the fresh pain and isolation of your family wound. When you feel misunderstood, you do not feel normal. You feel freakish. You feel negatively judged. These social situations can make you feel as if the unfulfilled need inside, begun by your toxic family, only grows deeper, as you feel a wedge developing between yourself and others in the face of their lack of understanding. To counter these feelings, give yourself permission for the following:

- You do not have to explain your decision about your family to others, beyond the basic facts.

- You can heal without predicating your healing on others' validating your choices.

- You can accept the love that people offer you and embrace it as valuable, even when they cannot fully relate to your story.

- You can be proud of the difficult decision you made to protect your peace from poisonous family dynamics.

- You can allow the painful family experiences you have lived through to be the only evidence you need to validate your decision.

You must come to expect that many will be able to *sympathize*, but fewer will be able to *empathize* with you or your circumstances. It will be normal to feel lonely on some level, no matter what and no matter who loves you, because so much of what you have gone through can be understood only within you, or by the rare kindred spirits who have had comparable experiences.

Invasion of Privacy

You are also likely to encounter the curiosity of others who sense you're keeping something about your family private. As they become more curious, they also become more invasive. No matter how well you try to maintain your privacy around this discussion, whether silently or directly, it often makes new acquaintances even more interested.

It is normal to dread this curiosity, because inquisitive people bring your vulnerabilities to the surface. I have always respected the need for privacy that I have sensed in others. I would never question them on a topic that would likely make them feel uncomfortable. Yet those trying to keep their family pain private often find that people who sense privacy around this topic rarely respect it. They ask questions anyway. These people usually do not *mean* any harm, but that doesn't mean their inquisitiveness doesn't *cause* harm.

Their invasiveness can feel uncomfortably similar to the invasiveness of the family environment you grew up in, raising your hackles. There is no such thing as respect for privacy in a toxic family. Your experience of being raised in a toxic family will naturally make you feel more self-protective around others and their inquisitiveness; however, this is healthy.

> **Moment of Insight:** You have every right to protect your story. If they haven't walked in your shoes, they can only pass judgment.

A great strategy when dealing with the nosiness of others and the void inside is to offer nothing more than superficial information about your childhood and knowledge of your family. To deflect the focus from your story, you can assume that most people love to talk about themselves. This makes it easy to turn the focus of the conversation to the other person by inquiring about *their* family or other personal details. It's easy to change topics and redirect the conversation to maintain your composure and privacy. If a person you are dealing with cannot control their curiosity and continues to push the subject, use a light approach: "Well, that's a conversation for a whole different time and place." Eventually it may be necessary to say, "It's not a pleasant topic for me, and one I prefer not to talk about much, but I appreciate your asking." No need to take on anyone else's feelings and opinions regarding your situation.

Hurting at Social Events or Gatherings

Social events such as holidays, weddings, birthday parties, anniversaries, and family get-togethers are prime times when the void of your family wound can be provoked, whether by your own family or the families of your friends or lovers. For survivors of family abuse, social events and gatherings tug on the natural need for family.

The new people you are spending time with and their extended family and friends are interested to learn more about who you are. Unfortunately, they also tend to ask questions about your family at the exact times of year these questions are the most tender for you emotionally. These interactions can trigger you into not wanting to do anything with anyone's family around holidays or other big events—a response you may need to manage. It is natural for new people to want to get to know you, and unfortunately major events are great conversation starters. Keep in mind that most people are not trying to bring up a painful topic for you.

> **Moment of Insight:** It is your right to keep that painful place inside safe from getting triggered, to protect yourself from your original pain growing even deeper.

That said, you still need to take care of yourself in whatever way is necessary around these times. For example, I choose to spend Mother's Day alone with my daughter. I do not spend it with other people and their mothers. It is not a day I want to be asked about my mother or be reminded of who my mother is as a mother or grandmother along with the endless abuses, gossip, and manipulations that continue to go on behind my back. On Mother's Day I make sure to celebrate the mother I am, the woman I am, the beautiful and close relationship I share with my daughter, and what an amazing human being she is. This helps me fill my emptiness rather than bleed from it.

I hope you can use this advice to tailor major events and gatherings to fit your needs. The social arena certainly wakes you up to the areas where the void of your family leaves you vulnerable in your life. It's a void that you must learn to fill in new ways.

> **Take a Moment for You:** Write down some changes you may need to make around social gatherings or holidays to better take care of yourself.

When you start developing relationships with new friends and lovers post cutting ties, you will face some deeply painful gaps where you realize pieces are missing that you never knew would be or could be missing until the empty spaces become evident. This only expands the void left by your toxic family members.

For example, many survivors face the fact that they'll never have the new people in their life observe them being loved and adored by family members, either privately or socially. When you observe your new friends or lovers being loved, honored, and adored by their own family members, it naturally adds to your idea of them, to your idea of the value they hold as a person, and to the love you feel for them privately. The more you bear witness to other people loving your favorite people, the more lovably you begin to view them. It is a magical thing.

Observing such interactions also helps you to trust your own social and internal judgment that you have picked a really good person to spend your time with. Unfortunately, when you enter a new relationship, the person you choose to love will never get to see you so embraced by the very people who should have been your greatest admirers and closest confidantes, your family. The new people in your life can never enjoy the kinds of inside jokes, playful banter, affectionate teasing, and meaningful conversations concerning you that really can come only from the family who raised you. You are missing some of life's most significant and fulfilling interactions nurtured by loving bonds, and so are the people who love you.

On a social level, nothing and no one validates our significance more deeply or firmly than family. But this is not the truth of *your* experience. It is simply a painful gap where a piece is missing, which adds to the depth of your void. This void is the new form of parent that you will be in a relationship with going forward. The void replaces their presence in your life, and there are ways to make this void livable and peaceful. Understanding the social environment is how we learn what the missing pieces are and learn to validate the gaps where they should be as places for us to grieve and then fill with a newfound energy of healing. Others will minimize your experience, but that has no bearing on the truth of your experience. You can learn how to hang on to what is true for you.

Minimizing Your Experience

There is truly nothing worse than having your pain over the estrangement from your family minimized by people in your social world who do not understand you. Whether you want the topic of your family to be wounding or not, it just is. How can it not be? It is strange how others view your life from the outside and assume that the loss of your family and the void it leaves is somehow no longer a daily issue for you. Yet because you have put the proper safeguards of separation in place, people expect you to be emotionally over it. After all, they reason, *you* were the one who cut ties with your family.

People with this insensitive and uneducated attitude have never swum in the waters you have almost drowned in. The painful decision to cut ties is one you'll need to think about and process on some level every day for the rest of your life. Your social network may have a hard time recognizing this, thereby unintentionally minimizing your pain. They also may not recognize the continuing hurt as your family members continue trying to sneak their abuses into your life.

When you get the "Aren't you over it yet?" response, or "How your family acts shouldn't surprise you," it is natural to question yourself. You grew up being manipulated to question your own version of reality, so to have this retriggered by others is hurtful. Because of how the brain is wired, the negative is always easier to believe than the positive. Negative thoughts are processed in a completely different part of the brain because they are bigger and harder to break down. For this reason, you must fight harder to feel your own sense of justice, forcing you to overexplain why you separated from the toxic family dynamic you lived in.

It would sure be nice if you did not have to go through this, but because family is so much of what defines any of us as a person on a social level, some of this is unavoidable. It is best to observe your social and emotional climate and learn to navigate it in such a way that you do not flounder in others' opinions, judgments, and minimizations. Understanding a concept I call the family "billboard" will help put you on track to protecting your internal world.

Dumping the Family Billboard

In social settings, when you are still in contact with your family members, no matter how minimally (with even one string attached), you do not have to deal with the scrutiny just discussed because you are, at the very least, carting around a billboard (metaphorically speaking) that says you belong to a family. Toxic families make sure their billboards present the most eye-catchingly healthy and normal front to deflect from the foundation of manipulation visible only within the family. When you are still connected to them, you may be tortured psychologically, but you have this billboard to protect you socially. In this situation you must be inauthentic, put on the fake smile, and pretend the false advertisement of your family is real. Hence, it is your *inauthenticity* that saves you from social scrutiny. How can this be healthy?

Understandably, you may stay in contact with your abusers because you feel safer with the false advertisement. In many ways it can be easier to live with false pretenses than to face the pushback of negative judgment from society at large. Completely understandable. Although it may be easier in some ways to live like this, I believe we are each hardwired to be authentic, to be individual, and to stand for what is right. As a healthy person you will be strongly drawn toward a path of living from truth, integrity, and accuracy.

When you have cut ties and no longer have a family billboard, *you* may not feel ashamed of this, but that does not mean others will not shame you for your choice to not have one. However, taking this step is a worthy challenge, because not having that billboard also frees you from the oppression and manipulation of your family, even though it sets you apart from others and alone on a path of not fitting in. As a survivor you know it is a lesser oppression to deal with the curious, naïve judgments and minimizations from others who mean very little in your big picture, than it is to live a false, meaningless, and tormented life with a destructive family.

Moment of Insight: When there is the will, there is always a way.

Standing Up to Pressures to Conform

People naturally judge what is different. I encourage you to walk boldly, understanding there is no life of legitimacy under the emotional slavery of a toxic family system. I love the words of Ralph Waldo Emerson: "To be great is to be misunderstood." It is your healing work to embrace the fact that if people who have not suffered what you have cannot accept the boundaries you have had to put in place in your life, they do not have to—but *you*, in turn, do not have to accept their false judgments. If you buy into these, you are allowing yourself to be fooled by the foolish. It can be painful to take a stand against these judgments, but I know from experience that it is possible.

Moment of Insight: Healing the wounds of misunderstanding comes not from getting others to understand you, but from having the courage to stand alone against all odds.

Author Brené Brown teaches, in *The Call to Courage*,[7] that our larger culture is always going to apply pressure to conform, and that unless you are willing to push back against that pressure and fight for what you believe in, your only other choice becomes living a life of scarcity. You're essentially giving up, based on the assumption that you are unworthy of more—of your own independent sense of self, separate from the family members who want to control and manipulate you. When you push back against the larger culture, Brown says, you are being called to dare greatly.

> **Take a Moment for You:** Reflect on what your life would be like if you dared greatly. What does daring greatly mean to you?

Cutting ties with your toxic family members is just such a choice. The path to living abundantly begins with the choice to face uncertainty, to take emotional risks, to be as you are in the midst of changing your life, and to believe that you are plenty capable of doing so. You will develop self-worth through a willingness to be brave enough to be yourself, regardless of how others may view you. It is less important to care about how others perceive you and what society deems socially and morally correct, and more important for you to feel good inside of yourself. This is a valiant move.

The Social Power of "Family" to Be You

Why does the topic of family so frequently enter the conversation with nearly everyone you meet? Because family is just that powerful when it comes to sharing who you are with other people. All people, including you, are a product of their family environment. On a psychosocial level, family identifies and defines you. People who want to know who you are and to expand their understanding of you delve more deeply into the type of family you come from. Knowing more about someone's family *does* help explain who they are. But allow me to remind you who you are: a *survivor*. A strong, brave, brilliant survivor of toxic family abuse.

It is when you decide to approach life bravely, to choose to be proud of your journey and thrive in your new chosen way of life—billboard free—that you start feeling inspired and alive again. You also naturally start inspiring others to live as their own best self. Your healing gives needed permission and approval to others, stuck in a situation like the one you've left, to consider taking better care of themselves. You can be an example of hope, especially when facing naysayers. Many people will not agree with your decisions to heal your life. This simply means you are not the right example for those particular people to follow.

Beyond the frustration you feel for being unfairly judged, you may discover hidden value in being misunderstood. It certainly makes life interesting and challenges your growth potential. Most important, it develops your resiliency. It is not always beneficial to have effortless understanding and security in life. Negative judgments are worthy obstacles you can overcome. *Yes, you can!*

I look at it this way: Giving birth is always difficult, but in going through the birthing process you are also creating greatness. If your baby stayed in the darkness of the womb it would never have the gift of seeing the light. This is also true of cutting ties with your dysfunctional family. Cutting ties is your rebirth. My own experience of being misunderstood gave me the courage to write my books, to offer readers a real, human example of being a survivor *and* a psychology expert who fully understands their journey. Because I have not just studied it as a clinical interest, but have lived and continue to live through the experience itself.

Here are ways to rebirth with courage:

- **Bring your fearful feelings into the light.** Whatever emotions you avoid feeling are the emotions you most need to examine. Bring them to light by writing them out, painting them, or meditating on them, or work through them by talking to a trusted friend or therapist. When emotions have a mirror (another person) or an outlet, they are more digestible.

- **Add emotional controls by taming the tendency to catastrophize.** Catastrophizing sabotages your mental health. It is hard not to get overly emotional when you feel more strongly than a situation calls for. Remind yourself that in this rebirthing journey, nothing is an emergency. If you feel you can't control your emotions, find some distance from others; conversation can and should wait.

- **Identify and name what you are afraid of.** When you feel fear, determine where it's coming from, then decide how real or rational your fear is and whether any action is needed to resolve or calm it.

- **Envision the positive outcome of facing this fear.** When you feel paralyzed by fear, turn that negative vision around by imagining the more positive outcome you want to happen. Then put that positive outcome on repeat in your mind until it becomes your reality.

- **Generate a belief in yourself as totally capable of quelling the fear.** When you feel a fear is insurmountable, imagine seeing yourself conquering that fear. How do you feel as you face the fear? Now imagine how you would feel after successfully defeating that daunting situation. If you can dream it, you can achieve it.

- **Take the leap and confront your fear head on.** Having rehearsed this in your mind, when your imagination meets reality, it's time to act on what you have rehearsed. Mental rehearsal is almost as good as actual practice, because now you know what you are capable of doing. Fear gives you the opportunity to be your own hero.

- **Build your tolerance of fear by facing fears little by little each day.** Facing fear is a daily practice. When you conquer facing smaller fears, such as saying no to an unappealing invitation, you gain the confidence to face larger fears, such as setting boundaries on the toxic people in your life. Never wish for a life free of fear, for without it you cannot grow.

You don't owe anyone your attention, loyalty, or love if they are abusive. This includes your family and others in your broader social circle. It is not your responsibility to be loyal or loving to people who have abused, mistreated, or socially shamed you—especially when these people continue to ignore what you feel and the healthy boundaries you have set. If the people who are hurting you say they are trying to help you, that does not in any way make them an exception to this rule. You can set boundaries with the larger social world and teach everyone that you will stand up for what you know is right for you. They can accept it or move on. Once you accept that it is your right to do this, you can begin to heal.

PART 2

your
personal
healing
is now
possible

Chapter 6

The Core Wounds of Self-Doubt and Unworthiness

Without your family members' consistent negative influence on you, you gain the psychological space to grasp the origins and intensity of how you came to live with the pervasive, nonproductive mindset that you are not good enough. You were raised in a family that made you feel doubtful of your every move, thought, deed, action, reaction, and emotion. The depth of your family's manipulation had and will continue to have a hold on you, one that you may fear will never break.

As counterintuitive as this may sound, the self-doubting belief that you are not lovable or acceptable will resist your efforts to heal.

When any pattern resists being given up, it is considered a "syndrome." Survivors of toxic families suffer from the "not enough" syndrome, which is driven by self-doubt. Negative beliefs about yourself will cling tightly, because your value has been based solely on making other people happy and keeping the peace even while often being accused of being the problem. You likely have learned to apologize even when you have done nothing wrong. On some level, you feel you can never be good enough to please, or gain praise from, people you love. Therefore you conclude you are not enough.

Moment of Insight: People pleasers often start off as parent or family pleasers.

When nothing you do as a child to secure a feeling of love and safety from your family works to bring you the connection you deserve and need, you become wounded at your core. You begin wondering what is so bad about you that the people whose love should be a given in your life express no love for you. This is a core wound.

Understanding Core Wounds

When you separate yourself from family, your psyche leaves this dynamic with permanent scarring—the marker of a core wound. Core wounds develop when the actions of someone you are extremely close with, such as a family member, cause you intense emotional pain—so intense it damages your very soul. Core wounds show up as feelings such as these:

- *I am not good enough.*

- *I am not lovable to my parent or other significant family members.*

- *I am weird, stupid, unwanted, a burden, alone, ugly [the list goes on].*

- *I am either too much of something bad or not enough of something good.*

Regardless of your exact core wounds, I can guarantee they influence who you are and how you behave every single day.

Take a Moment for You: Write down your core wounds. Describe how they feel and record examples of how they affect your daily life. This may help you step back enough to start seeing that these wounds were inflicted on you and have nothing to do with who you really are.

Self-doubt can paralyze you enough to stop you from anything and everything you want to feel, believe, and accomplish, which serves to keep you reliant on your family. A primary goal of any toxic family is to allow no member to escape the circle of dysfunction. This is achieved by deliberately creating insecurity.

Toxic shame and doubt are not hard to create in children, given their inherent vulnerability, still-developing brain, inexperience, and dependence on family. Through my own healing I've learned that the "bad behavior" of a child in a toxic family system is more than likely a healthy, natural reaction to antagonistic emotional games. Unfortunately, when you were a child there was no way for you to conceptualize this. In toxic family systems, emotional games are used in lieu of the time, love, attention, parenting, or bonding required to make children feel healthy and secure. Because of this deep insecurity, you leave childhood inexperienced in love, highly experienced in fear, and feeling deeply ashamed of who you are, with no understanding as to why. It is essential to understand the whys of the person you have become.

> **Moment of Insight:** Healing core wounds starts with your efforts to rewire the way you think and feel about yourself.

Deprogramming psychological abuse is a critical step in your healing. Brush past this step, and the lies you have been told about who you are will continue to hold you hostage to your feelings of insecurity long after you have separated from your abusers. Deprogramming involves unpacking the trauma that created your core wounds. You must identify your abusers and examine the lies they programmed you to believe about yourself so you can start telling yourself a more honest narrative.

Nearly all toxic families have some level of dysfunction at the top—in the parenting. Toxicity typically starts with or is enabled by your leaders. Not all toxic adults had toxic parenting; other factors—such as addiction, mental illness, and genetics—can create toxic adults when the parenting has been good enough. However, most of those who become abusive and manipulative as adults do grow up with a toxic parent or guardian. Here are some examples of family systems that perpetuate core wounds through the generations:

- Some parents prefer one child to another, thereby creating conflict.

- Parents of toxic families thrive on the divide-and-conquer paradigm to create insecurity and maintain manipulative control over all family members, nuclear and extended.

- Some parents overly enmesh with and live vicariously through their children.

- Some parents overly control and criticize their children.

- Some parents abuse, neglect, and abandon their children, or resent having to be responsible for them.

- Other parents become jealous of their children, seeing them as unwanted competition.

- Many toxic parents program their children to feel they "owe" the parents anything and everything; even after boundaries have been set, they will claim personal rights to the personal lives of their adult children, including their grandchildren, on which they should not have any claim. (Children should be raised to be set free, not raised to be kept a prisoner to parental demands.)

- Some parents do a little bit of some or all of these things.

For all these reasons and more, love becomes a painful and confusing topic for survivors, far past childhood. Thus examining your upbringing and parenting helps you understand how your family's dysfunction has impacted you, the insecurity it has created around your self-perception, and the conflictual relationships you may have with your other family members.

Your psychosocial development affects your self-worth. As Susan Forward describes in her book *Toxic Parents: Overcoming Their Hurtful Legacy and Reclaiming Your Life*,[8] like a chemical toxin, the emotional damage inflicted on a child by their family spreads through the child's whole being, and as the child grows, so does their emotional pain. This pain and its long-lasting impact can be more fully understood by looking at how we develop socially and emotionally as children. The psychosocial theory of life span development developed by Eric Erikson[9] can show you how, when, and why your crippling feelings of self-doubt were created. His theory shares how and why the emotional damage done has such a lasting impact throughout life. In my experience, once a person understands how, why, when, and where the damage happened, this knowledge places them more securely on the path to recovery.

Self-Doubt Starts in Infancy

This first stage of life runs from birth to eighteen months. This is when you learn that either you can trust your parents/caregivers and the larger world around you or you cannot. If the care you receive is consistent, predictable, and reliable, you can develop an innate sense of trust that your critical needs (for being fed, cleaned, held, soothed, protected) will be met. By developing trust in infancy, you also develop the virtue of hope. (Erikson uses the term "virtue" for a number of positive attributes beyond the older theological concept.) Hope is founded in the understanding that as new challenges arise there is a real possibility that other people will be there to act as sources of support.

However, if the care you receive is inconsistent, unpredictable, and unreliable, you will develop mistrust. Growing up in a psychologically dysfunctional family, you likely failed to acquire the important virtue of hope, because you failed to develop trust. When hope is not developed, it is replaced with fear.

It is easy to see how the seeds of self-doubt are planted in this very first stage. In this stage, your voice is the sole resource for getting your critical and basic needs met. If your cries for nurturing went largely unmet, or if caregivers met them with an agitated frustration at having to take the time and effort, you learned that using your voice did not have the power to influence events or get your basic needs met safely or predictably. This general sense of mistrust created anxiety and a heightened sense of insecurity at this most vulnerable age, causing you to feel chronic feelings of uneasiness and apprehension.

While you cannot remember these early stages, because they are pre-verbal and precognitive, they are not *prefeeling*. You can look at some basic evidence to imagine how successfully, or unsuccessfully, you passed through this stage.

Take a Moment for You: Reflect on the following questions and respond to them in your journal. Go beyond simple yes or no responses to describe how these experiences play out in and affect your life.

- Do you live with a deep feeling of uncertainty about love and relationships?

- Do you believe you can count on people to support you in times of duress? Or does it feel like you must get your needs met on your own?

- Do you over-function in life and/or relationships to alleviate fear and anxiety?

- Do you believe your voice has the power to influence others?

- Do you live with a positive feeling of hope most of the time, or with a feeling of fear?

The Effects of Insecure Attachment to Caregivers

If you had emotionally disconnected parents who were too preoccupied to appropriately or healthfully connect with you, it's likely you did not form a bond with or attachment to them. In your early childhood, this lack of available or normal, healthy, connected care and attention from your parent (or primary caregiver, if biological parents did not raise you) can cause problems in your mood, behavior, and social relationships that psychologists call *attachment disorders*. Attachment disorders start developing in the first stage of life and continue to develop as we age. Because the first stage of life is when you establish your foundation of trust necessary for healthy attachment, it makes sense this is also the time when attachment disorders develop. I'll describe the different attachment styles so you can more thoroughly examine and understand which style or styles most relate to you. This will help you define and identify the way in which you learn to form healthy, secure attachments today, as an adult.

Secure Attachment Style

If you had been fortunate enough to have emotionally connected parents, you would have come through Erikson's first stage of life securely attached to them. Being securely attached would indicate you had parents who met your basic needs, which set you up to start life with an inbuilt assurance to act independently and with the belief that people are supportive, available, and trustworthy. Note: children can be securely attached even when they have just one parent attuned to their needs. Many single moms and dads raise securely attached children.

Securely attached children grow into adults whose confidence is natural and authentic—not something they gain and lose based on life challenges with any extreme. They will certainly feel their confidence wax and wane, but for the most part their confidence is stable across situations and environments. Not so for those of us who were raised by emotionally self-absorbed parents.

There are *insecure* types of attachment; let's explore the main types.

Disorganized or Disoriented Attachment

Disorganized attachment is typical when you have suffered some type of abuse in childhood. For example, you may have been left alone without support during critical moments of distress, or your primary caregiver may have used emotional or physical violence, or intimidation, to punish or threaten you into good behavior. Caregivers in this category do not show love toward you so much as they exhibit an uncaring and frustrated attitude. You get the sense that your caregivers could take you or leave you, which leaves you feeling unwanted.

My father had the classic Jekyll-Hyde personality. I never knew, and to this day could not accurately predict, whether he was going to be fun, or whether that fun would frustrate him and he'd switch into his emotionally and physically violent mode. I certainly have more memories of being afraid around him than of being at ease. He hit us, yanked us, and pushed fun (tickling or wrestling) to a point of physical discomfort; he would become enraged at the drop of a hat. Further, he used odd natural health theories to manipulate and control, putting my body, mind, and emotions in unsafe places. He abused my body by forcing me to take horse pill–sized laxatives when I was too young, for some random health benefit. Eventually the laxatives caused me to bleed when I went to the bathroom, but I was too afraid to tell anyone, especially him. The healthy balance of my digestion was destroyed, and I missed many days of school due to horrible stomach pain. When my father saw I had nearly all failing grades in my classes, he made sure to tell me what a failed mess I was. I believed him.

Moment of Insight: When children cannot understand or find answers to what is happening to them, they will automatically believe that it is their fault.

When Karina was very young, too often she was left alone with her younger brother at far too young an age so her mother could go out with friends, party, and date different men. Karina was left to be the adult in the house. She has a memory of calling her father in the middle of the night when she realized her mother still had not come home, feeling terrified and scared her mother had died. Her mother had not died; she had passed out and stayed the night at someone else's house. Her father came over and took Karina and her brother to his house. Her mother later punished her for calling her dad.

Take a Moment for You: Reflect on some examples from your own childhood of abuse, confusion, fear, or neglect. Record them in your journal to see if this attachment style is something you resonate with.

Anxious-Ambivalent Attachment

At the root of the anxious-ambivalent attachment style are contradictory parents. Being raised under this type of parenting, you never knew what to expect from one minute to the next. For example, in my household my parents both married and divorced multiple times, with much dating in between. My sibling and I met most of these different people. My father was out of our life more than in, but when he was in our life it would feel like a torrential hurricane had passed through, because he always brought drama and conflict. He came and went of his own accord, but we were expected to treat him consistently as our dad.

My dad constantly exposed us to bizarre spiritual beliefs in tandem with his natural health "antidotes." After a "spiritual reading" he participated in, he shared with me that I was his lover in past lifetimes, which was a horribly violating, confusing, and inappropriate thing for a father to say to his daughter. He told me my mother did not like me in this lifetime because she was still jealous from past lifetimes where he always chose to have me as his lover over her. The distorted narcissism in him made me feel deeply anxious, ambivalent toward him, and horribly uncomfortable. I never knew if he loved me, how he loved me, or if he did not care about me at all. I was confused about whether my mom really hated me and if it was because of my dad's choosing me over her in past lifetimes. I was too young to decipher what any of this meant—or to consider whether it could simply be pure fiction.

My mother, on the other hand, put her romantic relationships before her children and would try to make up for it by telling me that whenever I felt alone she was "like Jiminy Cricket, sitting on your shoulder, always with you." A pretend Jiminy Cricket was a poor substitute for a mother. My mother was either warm and lively or cold, petulant, needy, complaining, sick, and exasperated, making me feel insecure and agitated around her. Her self-preoccupation consumed her.

Jack grew up in a family where his father was more of a dictator over the whole household than a father. Jack's father demanded a clean, quiet, and perfectly organized home that was not conducive to the activities of normal, healthy, rambunctious children. Jack was always terrified that he might do something that would set off his father into a full-blown, terrifying rage that made no sense to a child. Jack understood that he was to be seen but not heard. This plunged Jack into fear. Jack learned to not be himself around his father, to keep himself safe from the lack of predictability and looming emotional violence. To this day Jack claims that when he is around his father he feels ambivalent. His body stiffens and he becomes very quiet. This ambivalence is reflexive, putting him on high alert to tread lightly.

Take a Moment for You: Reflect on some examples from your own childhood of ambivalence or unpredictability. Record them in your journal to see if this attachment style is something you resonate with.

Through these examples, perhaps you can come to understand why you grew up feeling anxious and ambivalent, first around your family members, and later in life with others. When everything about your family's behavior was contradictory, hurtful, and unsettling, it led you to live with feelings of intense fear, confusion, and anxiety, rather than from hope or trust.

Anxious-Avoidant Attachment

The prominent feature of the anxious-avoidant attachment style is distant and emotionally unavailable caregivers. Commonly, these parents justify their lack of parenting with the excuse that their distance will push you to be independent and responsible sooner. As you grow up, you may appear independent to others, but at your core you may be living in an extreme state of anxiety when you feel someone is getting too close to you emotionally. Further, because you received so little emotional connection from your caregivers and no one showed you appropriate ways to speak or behave—a helpful model called *mirroring*—you may find it hard to recognize, label, communicate, and express your emotions when asked to describe them.

Two examples of this attachment style come to mind: Richard, a police officer, and Lisa, a retired firefighter. They each grew up in families where the parents did the minimum amount of parenting to produce the most independent children. In adulthood, they each married and divorced toxic spouses; they have been single for nearly a decade. Both Lisa and Richard feel mentally and emotionally jumbled and incapable of explaining or expressing their thoughts, feelings, or ideas. They express intense confusion when trying to decipher whether what they are feeling is right, wrong, crazy, understandable, or reasonable. Both are voracious readers and researchers. They look for resources to help identify and validate what is going on inside of them. Because Richard and Lisa had little to no psychological mirroring, since their caregivers were so absent, they are afraid of people and do not trust themselves to read their emotional environment correctly. Richard and Lisa prefer being alone to exposing themselves to the risk and ambiguity that is natural to healthy relationships.

Take a Moment for You: Reflect on some examples from your own childhood of distant or emotionally unavailable caregivers. Record these in your journal to see if this attachment style is something you resonate with.

Each of these insecure attachment styles comes with its own layers of trauma, which create a lifelong deep sense of wounded insecurity and a lack of trust when it comes to relationships. This type of wounding impacts every relationship or attempted relationship you may have.

Your Core Wound's Impact on Love

In dysfunctional family dynamics, healthy love is not given or received, and that lack of healthy love is often detrimental to how you approach love. In most cases, our main forms of loving as an adult arise from what we needed but did not receive as a child. You may love people out of the need to be loved in return. Or when you love someone, you may try to use this love to fill the depths of the emptiness you feel in your soul. On the other hand, you may try to avoid love altogether.

All of this makes sense when you understand how you learned to attach to people. When you love, you love from your wound rather than from security. That core wound causes you to live feeling afraid of losing love and terrified of the peril that will put you in. It's easier to feel confident and happy when you are being loved, but if or when that love ever goes away, you quickly lose your grip on yourself and feel utterly unlovable and lost. Each time you lose love, even when it is your choice to end a relationship, perversely it somehow confirms your deepest fear that perhaps your family was right about you: you are impossible to love. Or you conclude that the love others feel for you is not strong, deep, or meaningful enough to inspire them to do the work it would take to create an enduring relationship with you.

> **Moment of Insight:** When you are insecurely attached, your deepest fear is that you are not deserving of the kind of love that is worthy of another's time, thought, effort, or commitment.

Living with this pervasive insecurity that impacts every part of your life is incredibly challenging. The world is unpredictable enough without such issues around love and attachment. A sense of community is positively correlated with happiness, yet how do you connect with others when you are afraid of love and attachment? It helps to understand where the strong, ongoing anxiety you experience originates so you can work to heal it.

Living with Foundational Anxiety

With your manipulative and abusive family dynamics, you probably live with feelings of anxiety. This unconsciously flows from the absence of safety and predictability—and the abundance of insecurity, uncertainty, and confusion—that you felt throughout your upbringing. When I was trying to understand the type of anxiety I was experiencing, I couldn't find it described in the *DSM-5* or in any of the psychology literature. I identified with certain criteria in the research or diagnoses for anxiety, but nothing clear enough to encompass what I was experiencing. So I have coined my own term that I think will also be helpful for you: "foundational anxiety."

Foundational anxiety is not a brain chemistry issue but rather an attachment issue. When your core attachment foundation is unstable, so are you. Susan Forward teaches that "an unpredictable parent is a fearsome god in the eyes of a child. As children we are at the mercy of our god-like parents. If we never know when the next lightning bolt of neglect, abuse, or manipulation will strike, we live in fear. The fear of its strike and the anxiety of not knowing when it is going to hit becomes deeply ingrained and grows in us as we grow."[10] This anxiety during development led to shame and self-doubt that began growing before you even had the capacity to understand it was happening.

> **Moment of Insight:** "Every formerly mistreated adult, even high achievers, is a little child inside who feels powerless and afraid."[11]

Science and Attachment

Without scientific proof of how attachment works, survivors are left with only subjective theories that do not necessarily validate their experience in a way that seems provable to the larger society. For this reason, I want to move beyond psychological theory into a brief discussion of scientific theory.

> **Moment of Insight:** When you can prove theories about yourself to be true with scientific evidence, you increase your own confidence that what is going on inside you is real.

In a study titled *Fear In Love: Attachment, Abuse and the Developing Brain*,[12] researchers demonstrate that wounding and traumatic experiences in childhood do impact the brains of children. Evidence supports how profoundly an emotional disconnection between parent and child influences the way your brain reads and uses genetic material as you mature. While researchers are less certain about how these early life experiences change the brain, they do know the brain responds by changing its structure, gene expression, and function.

The remarkable book *The Body Keeps the Score* by Bessel van der Kolk supports the theory that children have a biological instinct to attach.[13] Whether your parents or caregivers were loving and caring or distant, insensitive, rejecting, or abusive does not matter. You will develop a coping style that is based on your attempt to get at least some of your needs met. As a child, you had no control over how your genetics responded to the need for attachment. Van der Kolk teaches that "terror increases the need for attachment, even if the source of comfort is also the source of terror."[14] You had to seek attachment with your caregiver, even though you received only occasional benefit or were rejected altogether.

Van der Kolk's research further shows that the uncertainty you lived with had a marked impact on your stress system. How can any child feel safe enough to relax when no one is protecting them? Even long after childhood is over, your stress response is easily reactivated at the slightest hint of danger. The stress response sets your disturbed brain circuits in motion, secreting massive amounts of stress hormones into your system. This manifests as unpleasant, painful feelings, intense physical sensations of being nauseous or sick, shortness of breath, and an increase in blood pressure that often leads to aggressive or impulsive actions. You experience these reactive moments as panic; life and love seem incomprehensible and overwhelming, leaving you feeling out of control and depleted. These reactions, coming from a traumatized brain, are the basis of foundational anxiety. Trauma occurs when you have been placed in environments or situations of overwhelming stress that at that time were beyond your coping capacity. That made it impossible for you to assimilate the emotions involved that could help you repair. This lack of assimilation leads to the lifelong consequences of core wounds. Trauma is forever held in the deeper recesses of the brain. This is why trauma can be so easily triggered.

The following table highlights the differences between a traumatized brain and a healed brain.

Traumatized Brain	Healed Brain
Always on alert, fearful	More relaxed, trusting
Cynical outlook	Optimistic perspective
Fixed thinking	Open mind
All-or-nothing viewpoint	Sensible viewpoint
Scarcity mindset	Possibility mindset
Fear of being judged	Self-confidence
Guilty until proven innocent	Innocent until proven guilty
Attacks first, asks questions later	Avoids assuming, asks first

From these lists, you can see how tremendously different a healthy brain is from one that has borne significant trauma. Thankfully, though you were raised in trauma, this does not have to be the permanent way in which you approach life. There are ways to start healing your brain.

Moment of Insight: While it's discouraging to know that trauma changes the brain, remember that healing can change the brain too.

To heal emotional trauma, you can begin examining pertinent memories from your childhood for their significance and witness how they activate your stress system. Memories that continue to affect you are known as "emotional triggers," and you can identify them by the accompanying feelings of fear, shame, and self-doubt. Emotional triggers include, but are not limited to, memories, experiences, events, conflicts, or anxieties that set in motion intensely felt reactions, regardless of your current mood. The self-reflection questions I offer, begun in this chapter and continued in the next chapter, guide you to identify your emotional triggers. In later chapters you will learn how to repair them.

Chapter 7

How Toxic Shame Develops

Toxic shame is the devastating experience precipitated by the trauma you endured. Toxic shame starts developing in the second stage of life (described shortly) and continues as you age.

In my family, I was the outcast. I was able to sense very early the dislike that my family, specifically my mother, had for me. I was treated as an annoyance, and the disdain for me quickly spread to other members of my family, who without question judged me as "not well." (This has continued beyond my childhood; most of my adult life has felt like a witch hunt.) I was regularly used, abused, and scapegoated.

The pain of this was incredibly damaging to my self-worth, my relationship choices, and my overall view of life and people. I believed I was bad, damaged, a burden, and "not well," because that was the consistent message I received—in essence, I felt ashamed of myself.

Toxic shame is experienced as persistent, irrational feelings of worthlessness, humiliation, and self-loathing. Feelings of shame cut deeply into the human psyche and are powerful enough to paralyze your ability to think rationally. Toxic shame can strike unexpectedly from the slightest trigger, making you feel emotionally hijacked, unable to regain control over your emotions and reactions. Unfortunately, this inability to self-manage only leads you to feel more shame.

Toxic shame isn't the end of the world for you. Is it a painful can of worms to open? Yes, it is. However, it is also where you start seeing the truth through the lies. Therefore I encourage you to open this can of worms and dive in. The truth is there, along with your healing—and a sense of peace. When shame no longer has you in its grasp, your life will change significantly for the better.

Autonomy Versus Shame and Doubt

Stage two of your psychosocial development, as Erikson describes it, covers ages one and a half to three. You are called to master your first tastes of independence and the feeling of being a separate person from your caregivers. It is also the stage when you are most vulnerable to developing feelings of shame.

During this time, you are supposed to be developing the virtues of confidence, determination, and exercising will (in Erikson's description, discovering autonomy and doing things for yourself). Erikson states, "It is critical that parents allow their children to explore the limits of their abilities within an encouraging environment that is tolerant of failure. If children are criticized, overly controlled, or not given an opportunity to assert themselves, they begin to feel inadequate and to feel a sense of shame or doubt in their abilities."[15] When a child passes through this stage healthfully, they develop this idea: *I can rely on myself.*

When you do not pass through this stage healthfully—whether you were severely punished for exerting yourself, insulted when you tried and failed, or even laughed at when you persisted in trying to get your needs met—shame takes root within you. Shame is perhaps the most destructive of all the emotions, because shame does not go away on its own. As you grow to adulthood, you may seek to rid yourself of shame in several ways. You may blame other people for your circumstances or the consequences of your actions, which can lead you to display the traits of a narcissist. Perhaps you, like your toxic family, can suffer from immaturity, continuing to throw childish tantrums into adulthood. On the other hand, if as a child you were naturally more empathetic in response to your dysfunctional parenting, you likely internalized the shame you felt, convincing yourself that you were the source of your parents' problems, which led you to blame yourself.

There are three ways to leave the second developmental stage:

- With a healthy sense of autonomy

- With an egocentric narcissism, whereby you blame others for your problems

- As a self-deprecating empath, whereby you blame yourself for everything and seek to please others

Take a Moment for You: Reflect on the following questions and respond to them in your journal. Go beyond simple yes or no responses to describe how these experiences play out in and affect your life.

1. Were you raised in an environment that was tolerant of failure?

2. Did you feel encouraged to explore and test boundaries? Or did you have to either rebel against rigid rules or acquiesce to them?

3. Do you currently live with a sense of adventure, or do you fear getting out of your comfort zone?

4. Are you allowed to be independent as an adult, or do your family members pressure you to meet their needs and not separate from them?

5. Do you have memories of being shamed, humiliated, or criticized?

6. Can you make decisions on your own, or do you need your opinion validated by other people before exercising your will?

Keep your responses at hand, because by gaining clarity on how you developed during this stage, you can begin to heal. If you entered this stage without trust and left this stage feeling ashamed, that made what came next even harder. From here on, shame only grows to more profoundly impact your life.

Initiative Versus Guilt

Erikson's third stage spans the ages of three through five. This stage is about being purpose-driven. You are learning to apply more inventiveness and creativity to your independence. You are becoming less self-centered and more social. Given the opportunity to explore your ingenuity, you develop a sense of initiative and feel secure in your ability to lead others and make decisions. Conversely, if your moves toward taking initiative are squelched, through either criticism or control, you develop a sense of guilt and shame over your desire to lead yourself and others and to become more separate from your family members. At this stage you also begin asking many questions, as your thirst for knowledge is growing. If your parents treated your questions as trivial, annoying, embarrassing, or irritating, you will have developed feelings of guilt and humiliation for being curious.

If you had healthy parenting at this stage, you will have developed the virtue of determination. When you are raised in a destructive family system, taking initiative is its own unique kind of treachery. I and many of my patients carry memories of being given a look of disgust. In psychological literature, this is called the "narcissistic stare." This stare or look of disgust was likely one of your family members' most lethal weapons, giving you the message that you are not worthy, shaming you to the core. They didn't need cruel words or physical punishment to show disapproval. A simple look of disgust was enough.

Too much guilt seeded during this developmental stage creates an anxiety that can make you slow to interact with others, which inhibits your creativity in this stage and beyond. It is easy to see how shyness develops in this stage, when you experience the fear of doing or saying something others do not agree with. Out of fear and projected guilt, you learn to say nothing. For children to feel some guilt is, of course, necessary, otherwise they would never know how to exercise self-control or develop a conscience. However, too much guilt takes away your initiative and feelings of belonging.

Take a Moment for You: Reflect on the following questions and respond to them in your journal. Go beyond simple yes or no responses to describe how these experiences play out in and affect your life.

1. Do you feel like a burden in your relationships with lovers, friends, or family?

2. Do you analyze everything you think, do, feel, and say?

3. Do you feel embarrassment or guilt when receiving gifts or compliments, but have no problem giving these same things?

4. Do you live life feeling as if you are walking on egg-shells, trying to please others to become someone they will like?

5. Were you or are you allowed to have your own voice and your own unique opinion, initiative, direction, or desires in your family dynamic? Do you have these qualities in your current relationships?

6. Do you avoid asking questions as a way to avoid looking "stupid" to others?

While I encourage you to embrace these reflection questions, I acknowledge that answering can be tough, as they bring up your feelings of shame and insecurity. But this kind of self-examination is worthy work. It will help you fully grasp how internalized feelings of shame and guilt have impacted you from the very beginning of your life. Understanding this concept will add direction to the way you analyze the rest of your developmental process and how you came to be the person you are today.

Industry Versus Inferiority

The fourth stage of life runs between ages five and twelve. The main task is to develop the virtue of competence as you build skills in areas that matter to you, your family, or society.

At these ages, many toxic family members overly value competence in external qualities such as grades, athletics, popularity, or appearance. In my case, appearance was and is particularly important to both of my parents. I have heard them endlessly shame people for their skin color and race, how they have aged, being fat, having a "gut," showing wrinkles, and on and on. It is sad for me to look back on my childhood and recall how many negative, cruel messages I heard, whether about other people or myself.

Critical messages about what competence means were programmed into your mind during this specific stage of development. When you leave this stage healthily, you develop the belief that you are capable. But if you didn't pass through this stage with empowering and encouraging messages, you likely developed unrealistic expectations around performance and feel discouraged from taking initiative because you doubt your own abilities and feel inferior to others.

Take a Moment for You: Reflect on the following questions and respond to them in your journal. Go beyond simple yes or no responses to describe how these experiences play out in and affect your life.

1. Were you supported and rewarded for your ideas or interests? Are you supported now?

2. Were you given the idea that you didn't measure up to some standard set by your parents?

3. Did you ever receive the message that you could achieve anything you wanted in life?

4. Did you feel you were loved as a person, or solely for how well you performed or how you looked?

5. Did you feel competent as a child, or inferior? What about now?

Feelings of inferiority come from the feelings of shame you experienced in early stages. One stage builds on the others, in terms of overall mental and emotional health or a lack thereof. Toxic family systems operate by making and/or needing others to feel inferior. These systems are not built around love. They are structured around who has power and who doesn't. Who is good and who isn't. For the system to function, those who don't have power need to remain powerless. This, however, is dysfunction. Your feelings of inferiority were likely programmed into you, rather than an expression of who you really are. The reflection questions are designed to help you see how the concepts of control and power operated in your life, and to see how that old program may be impacting you today so you can heal it.

Identity Versus Role Confusion

The fifth stage spans ages twelve to eighteen. During these years you are learning and trying on the roles you will occupy as an adult. Erikson suggests that two identities are developing in this stage: sexual and occupational. Throughout adolescence you are trying to discover who you are as a young person. You are determining your sexual orientation, exploring sex itself, what attraction means, and you begin thinking about romantic relationships.

When you come through this stage healthfully, you develop the virtue of reliability: committing yourself to others. This commitment holds space for, and is tolerant of, philosophical and moral differences between yourself and others. Failure to establish a sense of identity within your family or society sounds like this: "I don't know what I want to be when I grow up," "I don't know who I am," or "I am not loved or accepted for who I am." This leads to role confusion. Not knowing your place in the world brings on a host of negative feelings.

As a teenager without clarity about who you are, you may have developed eating disorders, engaged in promiscuity, or behaved rebelliously against family or social structures. When parents starve you of healthy love, encouragement, and acceptance, you learn to starve yourself of the same things. It makes sense that if a family is sick at the top (parents or caregivers), the trickle-down effect means the family will also be sick at the bottom (children). When you have been starved of love, in adulthood this will manifest in poor relationship choices, as you pick lovers, partners, friends, or work environments that starve you of the very things you lacked (support, guidance, reciprocation, acknowledgment, appreciation) in your toxic family environment.

Take a Moment for You: Reflect on the following questions and respond to them in your journal. Go beyond simple yes or no responses to describe how these experiences play out in and affect your life.

1. Were you condemned for expressing your anger?

2. Did you feel accepted for who you were?

3. Did you rebel against expectations as a teenager? Did you withdraw from becoming who you were told you were supposed to be? Did you avoid the responsibility of becoming who your family members pressured you to become, to not allow your power-hungry family members to have control over you and your direction in life?

4. As an adult, do you continue to rebel against expectations or withdraw from them?

5. Do you feel secure in who you are?

6. Do you feel confused about who you are?

It is normal to do the opposite of what you are told to do, be, or become when you feel you have no choice in the matter. It is a way of reclaiming the power of choice that should be yours. Looking back and seeing how young you were when your negative conditioning started, it's easier to understand why your "not good enough" feelings have always been so strong. How can you feel powerful if you have been raised to believe you are inferior? Whether you rebelled against the family, as I did, or you acquiesced and followed the rigid family rules, neither option will leave you feeling empowered. However, when I went through analyzing myself at these stages, I did start to feel empowered. I realized that I was the victim of a toxic system and that my insecurities and their subsequent behaviors were not the *cause* of my problems but rather a *symptom* of the dysfunction I was raised in. Allow this to inspire you. You were not the problem. The toxic system that molded your beliefs about yourself was the problem.

Intimacy Versus Isolation

Erickson's sixth stage runs between ages eighteen to forty. You are developing the capacity to give and receive love. You begin to share yourself more intimately with others, exploring relationships that lead toward longer-term commitments with someone other than your family. The successful completion of this stage is the development of the virtue of enduring love. Enduring love means that everyone involved is willing to work on themself and the relationship so that it can continue and love can flourish.

When you do not pass through this stage successfully, you may avoid intimacy and fear long-term commitments. Or you may feel desperate to cling and hang on to love, thereby suffocating it. Either way, you have learned that love hurts. Children raised in physically or psychologically abusive families are taught that love and abuse *can* coexist. This faulty belief unfortunately shapes your adult perceptions of love. You learned to cling to the belief that those who hurt you also loved you. Therefore, as an adult, you rationalize others' abusing or manipulating you as normal. In this situation, the shame you feel deep inside is reaffirmed by the people you choose to love as you grow up, causing your feelings of toxic shame to deepen and your view of yourself to plummet.

> **Take a Moment for You:** Reflect on the following questions and respond to them in your journal. Go beyond simple yes or no responses to describe how these experiences play out in and affect your life.
>
> 1. Do you fear a relationship's ending because you see it as abandonment?
>
> 2. Do you view love as weak and believe it crumbles under challenges and setbacks?
>
> 3. Can you trust other people to do the work a relationship takes? Can you depend on their willingness to resolve conflict?
>
> 4. Can you trust yourself to do the work required so love can continue in a relationship?

5. In your relationships, do you always have a plan B, anticipating what you will do if it doesn't work out?

6. Do you love yourself? Do you know if you are lovable?

The toxic family system manipulates your idea of love and intimacy, twisting and distorting it. Instead of relationships providing you with a sense of love or peace, they often make your protective walls go up; or conversely, you may find yourself feeling overly needy and uncertain about how to set proper protections in place to guard your heart. To heal the twisted version of love you grew up believing in, you must unpack your ideas of love and change them from twisted to truthful. When you can look at the truth of your beginning, you find more honest ways to relate to yourself and to the idea of love, and how to give and receive love with less fear.

Generativity Versus Stagnation

Stage seven runs from age forty to sixty-five. You have a strong desire to create or nurture things that will outlast you, often mentoring others or working to create positive changes that will benefit other people. You give back to society through the raising of your own children or nurturing others' children, being productive, and involving yourself in community activities and organizations. Generativity is a concern for the future and what you offer to the world; through it you develop a sense that you are a meaningful and significant part of the bigger picture of life. Success in this stage leads to feelings of usefulness and accomplishment, whereas a failure to give back leads to feeling a shallow and perhaps meaningless involvement in the world. Failing to find a way to contribute to others, you can become stagnant and unproductive. When you carry the enduring legacy of your toxic family into this stage, you feel disconnected or uninvolved in your community and within yourself, and separated from the larger society.

Take a Moment for You: Reflect on the following questions and respond to them in your journal. Go beyond simple yes or no responses to describe how these experiences play out in and affect your life.

1. Do you feel purposeless?

2. Are fear and toxic shame holding you back from succeeding in life as you would like?

3. How can you use what you have been through for good?

4. Can you see the flaws or the holes in your life as vessels for knowledge and personal growth?

5. Can you take control of your life now? If not, what is holding you back?

From my own experience, I know you can pass through this stage successfully—even after being raised in highly dysfunctional family dynamics. I have been able to turn my pain into my competitor, my mentor, and my inspiration. I have learned that it is completely up to me to write the ending of my own story. It is up to you to do the same, and you can!

> **Moment of Insight:** Family dysfunction trickles down from one generation into the next, like an avalanche, taking down and burying everything in its path. It continues until one person—you—decides enough is enough and finds the courage to turn and face the onslaught of abuse.

You can be this person who brings peace and psychological health to your own children and the generations to follow. Take what you have learned from your dysfunctional family dynamics and do something proactive and positive with those lessons. Turn your inner predators into a powerful sense of purpose.

Ego Integrity Versus Despair

As we grow older (sixty-five and up) and become senior citizens in the eighth stage of development, most of us tend to slow down our productivity and explore life as a retired person. During this time, you take inventory on your life and assess whether you feel accomplished or not. Success in this stage leads to the virtue of wisdom, which enables you to look back on your life with a sense of closure and completeness, which in turn helps you accept and approach the ending of your life more positively. Erikson believes that if you view your life as unproductive, feel guilt and shame around your past, or feel that you did not accomplish your life goals, you live this last stage of life feeling deeply dissatisfied—which leads to feelings of despair, depression, and, for many, deep feelings of hopelessness.

I can nearly guarantee that as your toxic family members approach their death, you will witness them descending into despair. They get progressively worse as they age and become increasingly bitter, because they valued the wrong things. They will end their life realizing there will be no U-Haul following their hearse with the money and status they may have accumulated. No one will honor their ability to control, use, abuse, and bully. The legacy they leave for those closest to them is not how loving they were or how good they made people feel. The legacy they leave is empty. They will end their life in a tantrum, still complaining that life and people were not fair and no one ever did enough for them, and with the distorted and false belief that they were the victim. They'll pass away finally knowing they were so cruel that members of their own family chose to cut ties with them.

Is this what you want for yourself? Absolutely not. You do not have to live your life or end your life feeling isolated, loveless, shut down, abused, in despair, or despondent.

Moment of Insight: You can make the choice to heal yourself and live in ways that inspire others to heal their wounds too.

It Is Never Too Late to Change

Changing may feel harder as you get older because your emotional triggers and feelings of shame are more ingrained. But that only makes healing even more rewarding. Let my story give you hope. I was in my late thirties when I felt able to start making the major changes I needed. I was acutely aware that I was repeating the shame-based dysfunction I was raised in. I hit rock bottom hard many times, went through divorce and family turmoil, and finally had to commit myself to thriving as a financially independent, emotionally healthy single mom. It was a painful, terrifying, humiliating, and lonely journey, but I did it.

> **Moment of Insight:** To find peace, sometimes you have to be willing to act with more agency and end your connections with the people, places, and things in your life that create a legacy of toxicity.

It became crystal clear to me that I had to face the reality of my unhealthy upbringing instead of continuing to be an expert at learning to function in my family's dysfunction. I did not want "functioning in dysfunction" to be my normal pattern with my family or anyone else. I wanted to live in a way that was emotionally satisfying. I want the same for you.

In the next chapter, we'll begin to chart that course for you, together. It starts with leaving toxic shame behind.

Chapter 8

Leave Toxic Shame Behind

From Erikson's theory of life span development, you can see that the deep toxic shame you feel at your core arose in the second stage of your life and continued its development since then. To cleanse your life of the crippling effects of toxic shame, you'll need to recognize shaming feelings when they arise. This is more challenging than it may sound. Often you cannot recognize when shame is active, because its presence has been and is normal in your everyday existence. To see something, you must first define it.

What is toxic shame? It's a poisonous mixture of painful feelings, including but not limited to regret, overwhelming apprehension, self-hate, humiliation, or feeling a complete lack of worth or personal value. Symptoms of toxic shame can influence all your thoughts, feelings, interactions, and behaviors. These symptoms include

- Low self-esteem and constant self-criticism

- Feelings of chronic worthlessness

- Self-sabotage

- Chronic and compulsive people pleasing

- Feelings of irrational guilt over things you are not guilty of

- Angry, defensive, pleasing, or avoidant behavior

- Settling for less than you want in career, relationships, and so on

- Imposter syndrome (*If people knew who I really am, they would not like me.*)

- Dysfunctional relationship patterns

- General suspicion or mistrust of people

- Shame anxiety—the chronic fear of being shamed

Sadly, shame is powerful enough to block you from experiencing the most beautiful emotional states life has to offer, such as trust, contentment, joy, freedom, love, fulfillment, creativity, and happiness. But I can tell you, from personal experience and also from the healing I have witnessed in clients, toxic shame can heal. We can become *whole* in who we are.

Toxic Shame Is Healed by Understanding Wholeness

The desire to experience a sense of wholeness is a natural and instinctual longing fundamental to the human experience. The concept of wholeness, however, is often misunderstood. Wholeness does not mean living in a perpetual state of well-being, happiness, balance, acceptance, peace, or love. That's utopia. Feelings of balance, peace, and happiness are wonderful, but they make up only part of what it means to be whole.

Wholeness, by definition, means having *all* the proper parts or components. To live from the wholeness of who you are, you must assimilate not just the good, but also the hard, sad, mad, scared, and angry aspects of who you are. Authentic wholeness includes the good and the bad, the resentments and the gratitude, the broken and the healed, the pretty and the ugly, the love and the pain.

> **Moment of Insight:** You deserve to be loved, especially in your less-than-perfect moments.

When you break down the concept of wholeness, it implies *substance*. Wholeness expresses the nakedness of your humanity. The greatest desire most of us have as human beings is to be loved for who we are as a *whole* person, rather than loved exclusively for whatever about us is more pleasing or desirable. But if you are *only* pleasing and desirable, you are not whole. You are presenting a partial and manufactured self.

Your Manufactured Self

Shame creates your manufactured self. Your manufactured self is experienced as a sadness or fear that brings on overwhelming emotional states of emptiness, futility, impoverishment, and loneliness. To find your way to wholeness, you can start by unpacking this manufactured self that you had to become to survive. To secure love, you had to pretend to be who and what you thought you were supposed to be, knowing that the rules on this would change from minute to minute based on the constantly shifting and unpredictable needs of your destructive family members. Because the abuse and manipulation were present from the very start of your life, you have never been given the opportunity to develop into the person you would have naturally become had you been raised in a healthier environment.

> **Take a Moment for You:** Reflect on how you have become a manufactured self: the part of you that becomes what you think others want, at the expense of your true desires.
>
> You get the chance to figure out who you are only when you are no longer connected to the poison of the family that compromised your well-being and personal development. However, even when you start living on your own, it is normal to habitually live subconsciously under their rule. You live trying to be good enough for everybody but yourself. The fears of what other people think and whether they approve of you can keep you a prisoner to being a pleaser: your manufactured self.

Fears of What Other People Think

To fear what other people think and how they will react when you tell them how you feel about them is second nature to you, coming from an emotionally abusive background. In a toxic family, you are ostracized and rejected for such honesty. Because this was your norm growing up, it makes sense that as you start the healing process, you will likely go through tortured internal emotional gymnastics, trying to make your communication with the important people in your life perfect to safeguard yourself from losing their love. I used to be so afraid to communicate with people I would feel physically sick beforehand. I had no experience or vision of conflict between myself and others ending in a place of mutual understanding. Conflicts in my upbringing always ended with my rejection.

Understandably, expressing your needs or concerns can become so scary that you end up not telling anyone at all. The sad thing is, this does not allow you to be seen, nor does it allow others to know what you need or how they can help.

Moment of Insight: Going against your authenticity causes you to live in resentment, while others have no idea you are even suffering.

Adam was raised by an extremely toxic mother, so he largely stays to himself, because he has a hard time trusting people and their intentions toward him. Adam has lived alone for years and has little interaction with his neighbors, even though they are on friendly terms. On one occasion, his neighbors invited him to their Super Bowl party. Adam was not a huge fan of either team that year, and ultimately what he really wanted to do was stay home and work on his house. This invitation to the party gave him tremendous anxiety. Adam worried his neighbors would see his car parked in front of his house and would either feel rejected by him or pass judgment on him, perceiving him to be a "weirdo-loner" because he wanted to be alone rather than at their party. To assuage his anxiety, Adam went against working on his house projects to watch a Super Bowl that didn't interest him at a bar some distance away.

Mind you, Adam is no wimp. He had a high-powered career in criminal law, working on many high-profile cases. In this moment, however, Adam's subconscious took over and hijacked him emotionally. He went against being his true self to avoid the judgment and rejection he projected that his neighbors would feel toward him.

The running dysfunctional theme for survivors is *If I don't do what other people want me to do, I will lose their love.* Sound familiar?

Take a Moment for You: Reflect on who you are and what your life and relationships would be like if you were true to yourself.

It takes a tremendous amount of emotional energy to constantly work to please others, be the perfect image of what they want, and do this knowing there is still no guarantee that pleasing anyone is even possible. It is exhausting. You may have experienced exasperated moments feeling like you just want to be yourself without fear.

The Search for Your True Self

As you are learning, to live from a place of wholeness, you must uncover the truth behind the unique story of your childhood. It is here, through this discovery process of your development, that you will come to rediscover your True Self. To be your True Self means you do not worry about pleasing other people or living by someone else's standards. You live as your natural self without compromise. However, it is important to be aware that the search for your True Self will likely awaken you to your pain before inviting you into the experience of relief from it. To uncover your True Self means clearing the cobwebs of the mistruths you were told about who you are and softening the defenses you have built to protect yourself from perceived or anticipated harm.

As I began unpacking my family's false and distorted narrative about me, I initially felt extremely angry. Their most prevalent lie, which I wholeheartedly believed, was that my family members were good and I was bad. I believed this lie because I was a child. Children believe what their family members tell them because they have no other experience to judge these lies against. "Bad" was the assumed role I was given in my family. I fit in as the perceived problem. Without a scapegoat (a person to blame and pick on), the toxicity in the family system cannot dominate. There must be at least one person to provoke and manipulate into carrying the outward expression of the trauma, so only they are seen as the cause of the family's problems. This setup relieves all other members of the family of responsibility for the consequences of their abuse. I did not choose this role, and I am certain you did not either. The scapegoat—the real victim—is deemed the perpetrator by the family, while the real perpetrators are seen as the victims.

Take a Moment for You: Reflect on what mistruths you believed about yourself, as assumed by your family members.

I challenge you to question what you think would have happened had you appeared before your self-consumed family members as needy, angry, truthful, confrontational, or furious. Where would your love from them have been then? Most survivors can attest to the knowledge that the love they needed would not have been available. They have expressed all of these varying emotional states and moods and been labeled the "problem."

Toxic family systems demonstrate an outright refusal to examine or acknowledge the pain they cause. You know from experience that your family members chose to ignore the pain behind your rage, neediness, truth, frustration, and sadness. They turned the tables on you, dismissing the validity of the truths you screamed. Instead of taking care of you or showing interest and concern for what you felt, they shunned you.

Sharon shared a story with me of how once, during a fight when she was a teenager, she told her mother she hated her, and to this day her mother still boasts that her response to Sharon was, "You may hate me, but I will always love you." Sounds good on the surface, right? What is hidden in that story is how deeply, spitefully, and intentionally Sharon's mother would provoke this exact negative reaction from Sharon. Sharon's mother provoked Sharon's hatred of her so she could flip the script and take the spotlight as "the good mother." Further, Sharon shared that her mother generally tells this story in some public forum, because her mother considers this a proud moment in her parenting.

It is the perfect way to scapegoat Sharon. Her mother enjoys creating the false narrative that she was a doting and unconditionally loving mother, and Sharon the horrible, hateful, out-of-control daughter, when nothing could have been further from the truth.

In Sharon's adulthood, when her mother has failed to accept or understand Sharon's feelings, the mother's response is a sarcastic "I just can't say or do anything right with you." This is scapegoating at its finest. Nothing about her mother's responses to Sharon's less-than-positive feelings has changed from childhood to adulthood. Thankfully, Sharon has come to realize that her emotionally manipulative mother responds this way any time an unpleasant truth about her mother has been raised for examination. These types of interactions are maddening. Unfortunately, this is the way they are.

It is not always difficult to *know* that your family members are toxic. The painful part is *accepting* that they are toxic; that this is who and how they are, and who and how they will be going forward. This reality creates deep feelings of loss and hopelessness, because accepting this marks the true end of your relationship with them. But just because you have accepted this disappointing and painful reality does not mean your emotional relationship with your family is over, even after having severed ties. Part of accepting your family for who they are is knowing you will always be connected to them emotionally, to the damage done, and to the longing for something different. The difference, after establishing no contact, is that you have put the relationship with your abusers into an *active state of emotional silence*. No more arguments, emotional games, manipulation, gossip, being ostracized, or defending yourself. No more verbal or physical engagement. This emotional silence largely mutes your predatory family's opportunity to continue to create chaos in your life.

Moment of Insight: It's healthier to adjust your life to the absence of your abusers than to adjust your behavior to accommodate their disrespect.

With ties severed, you have the space to search for, discover, uncover, and recover your True Self. You have the space to learn to be whole without shame and guilt. It is time to start giving the person you are today the encouragement you need and deserve for having come so far as an independent and resilient human being, despite the family that raised you.

Your Personal Rights

To find your way toward wholeness, toward your True Self, you must examine the pain and insecurity of your shamed manufactured self to start redefining your personal rights: those valid and necessary personal rights you have never established because you were not allowed this luxury. In toxic family dynamics, it is only when you smother your truth that you are met with tolerance. You can fit in only when you carry the responsibility for their abusive actions. You are forced to get on stage and play the role of the one who is dysfunctional. Over time, the shame of this role will so beat you down that you exist as nothing more than a hollow actor on that stage, slowly dying inside from your pent-up rage at the unfairness and hypocrisy of the game. Yet you follow the unfair rules, to keep your only sense of security: your family. Meanwhile, your family members gain adoration and praise for their Oscar-worthy performance: their perceived ability to deal with a difficult person such as yourself—and how hard and demanding that must have been for them!

Until you choose to step off that stage and discard the role you were forced to play, true healing is not possible. You cannot really love yourself if you are forbidden to be yourself. When you are on stage performing, you may fit in, but you are operating from your manufactured self. This part of you is confusing and deceptive because it is not real. On that stage, "being yourself" is about *performing* and *trying*, rather than *being* or *having*. The anger you feel toward them must be repressed in the presence of the family you fear, even as they are masquerading the illusion of love toward you. This insincere game is the birthplace of your insecurity. So step off that stage and take a stand for your personal right to be exactly who you are.

You deserve to feel free from the shame that was never yours to begin with. You deserve to feel important, significant, irreplaceable, and worthy. You deserve to be respected and to have your needs met. You deserve what you did not get.

Here are strategies for healing toxic shame, based on your personal rights as a human being:

- *Give yourself the time, love, and attention you never received growing up.* Take time for yourself in whatever ways you find nourishing.

- *Dismantle the manufactured self that is desperate to fit in, by being true to yourself.* Imagine who or how you would be if you weren't afraid of being rejected, or of not fitting in, or of people holding potentially negative judgments of you. Envision yourself being confident and fearless, and step into that vision little by little each day. One easy way to feel more confident is simply changing your posture. A slight lift to your chest and chin and a pulling back of your shoulders is proven to increase the chemicals in your brain responsible for generating a state of power and well-being.

- *Build self-worth by communicating your needs, wants, and emotions.* When you communicate these, practice stepping into your power rather than communicating from a feeling of being sorry that you have needs at all. Tell people what you need, politely but directly. Learn to use fewer words to get your point across. You no longer need to give a seminar on why you need something.

- *Recognize when you are working too hard in a relationship.* When you sense you are doing all the work in a relationship, stop. Back away and allow some space between yourself and the other person. In most cases the other person will notice and naturally begin making more effort toward you. If they don't, maybe this isn't going to be the right relationship for you, and that is okay too.

- *Remind yourself that you do not need to be perfect.* When you catch yourself in the anxiety of feeling like you need to be perfect, take a minute to recognize what is happening and add some soothing self-talk. Remind yourself that perfection isn't possible, nor is it required. Honestly, the more "perfect" you become, the less approachable you will appear to others. It is truly your imperfections that make you more likable, because they make you more relatable. It's no fun to be around a person who believes they are perfect.

- *Uproot and examine the triggered emotions and memories you reject and push down.* When triggers arise, let them come, and take some time to observe them. When a trigger is presented, there is always a learning lesson available. Triggers most often arise to signal that you may need to set a boundary. I suggest giving every triggered emotion twenty-four hours before deciding what course of action is best.

- *Work your way out of exploitative and neglectful relationships.* When you find yourself in a one-way relationship, this is a direct repetition of the toxic family that raised you. Notice what is happening, keep some notes so you can be sure, and start creating distance between yourself and the person you feel may be using you. Remind yourself that you deserve better.

- *Heal fears of being alone, which provoke you to conform and stay in unhealthy relationships.* It is scary and lonely to be alone, no doubt. However, you can be just as alone and even more miserable in an unhealthy relationship. So often, coming from family estrangement, we grasp at any relationship that can fill the void we feel inside. If you are alone, change your mindset to the idea that you are not *by* yourself, but *with* yourself. When you can enjoy your own companionship, you become less dependent on relationships as the only satisfying way to fill your cup.

- *Communicate feelings of disappointment, frustration, and anger.* It is your right and your responsibility to communicate with others. Relationships cannot grow, heal, change, or be nurtured without communication. You have to risk being vulnerable, which is scary, to establish relationships that work for you rather than against you. So say what you need to say.

- *Practice saying "Thank you," "I hear you," or "You may be right" in place of defensiveness.* Coming from a toxic family, where life felt like living in constant litigation, you may be more quick than others are to fall back on defensiveness. This is not so much about your not tolerating being wrong as it is about your experience of having lies about you seen as the truth—with your attempts to correct this proving ineffective. When you start feeling defensive, it's hard to know whether you are simply triggered or you actually need to defend yourself. To manage your defensiveness, you can practice saying "I hear you," or "I'm listening," or "Thank you for sharing," or "I will think about this." Then when you're in your own space you can work through your emotions, get clear on your position, and return to the person to share your insights.

- *Recognize your automatic response to shame.* When you feel a sudden intense onslaught of shame, you can bet you are triggered. Focus on stopping your thoughts from tumbling down the rabbit hole, where one negative thought builds on another and another. Shame can be stopped only when it can be examined. When you get ahold of your thoughts, they are easier to unpack and understand. Understanding puts you back on the path of healing.

- *Acknowledge the anxiety that leads to feelings of restlessness, and try to slow down.* Anxiety moves quickly, like a forest fire, spinning you out of control. When you start to feel anxious, allow yourself to feel it, while using self-talk to remind yourself that anxiety disrupts your ability to see clearly. Just adding this reminder to your self-talk is often enough to slow your anxiety down.

- *Replace shaming thoughts with their positive opposites.* Because you have been raised to have an abusive inner critic, you must commit to changing the way you talk to yourself, so you don't become the new abuser in your life. If you were your own child, how would you talk to yourself? If you wouldn't talk to your child in the way you are talking to yourself, then stop. Imagine how you would talk to your child, and apply that tone to the way you treat yourself.

- *Avoid shame reinforcers—those who criticize, belittle, and humiliate you.* If you want to feel less shame, you must identify the shamers in your life and remove them. Your inner critic is shaming enough. You do not need to keep shaming relationships or circumstances in your life. I promise that whatever you let go of will be replaced by something as good or better.

- *Release tension in your body through massage, exercise, yoga, or meditation.* So many survivors, coming from this type of family trauma, hold the pain of our emotions and experiences in the body through tension, often unconsciously. And many suffer from asthma, chronic headaches, stomach issues, sleep issues, sore throats, and autoimmune deficiencies. Practices that provide tension release help with all of these.

- *Openly accept and embrace love and kindness from others.* As hard as this may be, when kindness and love come your way, welcome them in. I believe that love is the answer for healing of any kind.

A simple truth: every child has a legitimate need to be noticed, understood, taken seriously, and respected by their family. When this was not your reality, you must learn to stand firm in who you are—in your needs to be noticed, understood, taken seriously, and respected by the people you choose to have in your life today. The mindset to hold is that you have paid your emotional dues when it comes to love. Make no excuse for abuse. Shift your perception from feelings of powerlessness to actively taking charge of your life's direction. You cannot go back and change what you did not get. However, you have the power to determine who is in your life today and how you choose to be treated.

I encourage you to become more honest, respectful, and conscious of who you are and the negative impacts your family has had. From this awareness, you can become less destructive in your own life toward yourself and others. Instead of ignoring what happened to you and allowing others to ignore it or excuse it away, open your eyes and the eyes of others to the vast damage done by a blatant double standard in the family system and society as a whole. The double standard is this: It is considered morally wrong to cut ties with our family, yet it is morally acceptable and even encouraged to cut ties with nonfamily abusers. People are people, and abusive family members shouldn't be given more power than any other abusive individual.

It is only when you speak your truth that you will know how to love and be loved. Learning how is no small task for those coming from a psychologically manipulative family.

Your twisted family dynamic has lifelong aftershocks. Part of riding out the aftershocks is learning to manage the impulse to leave relationships to protect yourself, when leaving may not be warranted. Conversely, you may need to work on not staying in unhealthy relationships—not tolerating disrespect far past the time you should. Or you may need to work on getting past the decision to abolish love and relationships altogether.

This space between staying, continuing to try, or going can be horribly murky, because you have not been taught to trust your instincts. The impulses—to stay too long, leave too early, or not attach at all—are a result of complex post-traumatic stress disorder (C-PTSD). Pete Walker, in his book *Complex PTSD: From Surviving to Thriving*, defines C-PTSD as a "severe form of post-traumatic stress disorder. This is the syndrome you develop when you do not pass through your psychosocial stages healthfully. Complex PTSD is delineated from the more well-known post-traumatic stress syndrome by five of its most troublesome features: emotional flashbacks, toxic shame, self-abandonment, a vicious inner critic, and social anxiety."[16] C-PTSD symptoms also include flashbacks, triggers, and core wound reactions common with other forms of PTSD. Let's look at these features of C-PTSD more closely.

Emotional Flashbacks

Emotional flashbacks are sudden and often prolonged declines into the overwhelming feeling-states of being abused, manipulated, or abandoned. This feeling states include but are not limited to overwhelming fear, shame, alienation, panic, rage, grief, and depression. When you feel overwhelmed with fear, you will feel extremely anxious and panicky; some may even feel suicidal. When flooded with feelings of despair, you may feel a profound sense of numbness, a physical inability to move (frozen), or the desire to hide yourself away from the world. No matter the trigger, you revert to a more regressive state of mind. When you are triggered, it is common to feel fragile, small, inexperienced, and completely powerless. These triggered emotional states are nicely frosted with doses of humiliation, crushing toxic shame, and thoughts like *What is so wrong with me?* or *Why am I like this?* or *Why am I so hard to love?* These deeply painful flashbacks take you to times you were shamed into believing you were not worthy.

Parental Contempt Leads to Toxic Shame

If, when you were growing up, your parents, siblings, or other family members reacted to your needs for love and connection with contempt or irritation, that will have caused you to feel deeply insecure and disconnected. Seeing contempt in the eyes and behaviors of family members is traumatizing for children and at best noxious to an adult. Contempt is a toxic cocktail of verbal and emotional abuse, denigration, irritation, disgust, or rage used to weaken and/or control others. A family member who rages is frightening. A family member who shows disgust toward you creates deep levels of shame. Shame taught you to stop asking for or seeking connection or attention from your family, because the rejection was simply too painful.

Self-Abandonment

These types of dysfunctional family dynamics thwart your need for bonding and acceptance, leaving you in fear (as an adult) that your needs for connection will never be met. Emotional neglect creates a similar pattern. If you were consistently ignored or shoved aside by your family, you were left to deal with unmanageable levels of fear and helplessness on your own and without support. When you engage in self-abandonment, you actively suppress, ignore, and reject who you are and your personal rights and needs. Because your needs were not allowed to come first, when you have a need, want, or desire, you decide not to satisfy it. It was your job instead to meet others' needs and standards as deemed important by the family system. The problematic combination of induced fear and shame leads to the development of your nagging inner critic—that abusive inner voice that holds you responsible for your own abandonment.

Vicious Inner Critic

Each of us starts life as the center of our own universe, where we interpret everything that happens to us from a singular view: our own. From this vantage point, it makes sense that if you are raised with love and encouragement, and to feel like the most lovable thing in the world, you will believe this to be true. You will believe this deeply enough so that when you encounter a message from the outside word that contradicts this belief, you will be outraged, because that negative message does not match what you have learned about yourself from your healthy upbringing. This outrage helps you maintain the original, positive self-image you were taught to hold.

When, on the other hand, you are raised in a poisonous environment, your sense of self is likely destroyed by feelings of contempt toward you, which makes you vulnerable to believing and fully assimilating negative messages from the outside world. Because of this internal match to the negative external messages, you likely won't protest when you're being mistreated, even when you know you should. The negative messages you're hearing now align with your inner critic, which started developing in your infancy.

> **Moment of Insight:** In a toxic family system, family members are absolved of the abuses acted out on you, while you become your own worst enemy.

Sadly, this self-critical and limiting way in which you have been raised to perceive yourself shapes your every relationship and interaction. When you are self-critical, you bear a host of negative labels that prove challenging to overcome when you look to dismantle them. The table compares the labels in a toxic family system to those in a healthy family system.

Labels from a Toxic Family System	Labels from a Healthy Family System
Bossy	Natural leader, imaginative
Defiant	Holds strong beliefs; daring, resolute
Demanding	Knows what they want; forthright
Dramatic	Expressive, enthusiastic
Fearful	Careful, discerning
Fussy	Has strong preferences

Hyperactive	Energetic, passionate, on the go
Impulsive	Spontaneous, intuitive
Oppositional	Advocates for a different perspective
Rebellious	Finding their own way
Stubborn	Persistent, determined, unwavering
Talkative	Enjoys communicating
Tattletale	Seeks justice, respects rules, fair
Unfocused	Multitasks, pays attention to many things
Attention-seeking	Advocates for needs, seeks connection

Moment of Insight: Negative labeling makes perfectly whole people believe they are broken. This is tragic.

Social Anxiety

When you grow up in a toxic family system, it's common to develop a deep-seated fear of people. Being emotionally abused creates a thick defensive layer around you, born of trauma and betrayal. This armor profoundly influences how you view people who desire to be closer to you. It is not that you are shy, playing hard to get, or being intentionally difficult in social situations. You are simply trying to protect yourself. You are often consumed with anxiety and worry about how others are perceiving you or misperceiving you.

Socially, it is often challenging to discern when to let your guard down or keep it up. I recommend both giving people the chance to earn your trust and holding back on fearfully judging them and their perceptions of you until they give you a reason to set boundaries. You can trust that with enough time spent around anyone, the truth of who they are will reveal itself.

Healing C-PTSD with the Three C's

What your family members did not provide *can* be gained in what many researchers refer to as *rewiring*—a great skill to master. For example, when you are in the throes of an emotional flashback, you can replace the negative inner critic with something more productive and positive. You can train yourself to use the Three C's Technique (catch it, check it, change it) to disrupt the negative tapes of your childhood.

When you feel yourself starting to decline into a regressed emotional state:

1. *Catch* your thoughts by recognizing you are thinking negatively. Once you catch the thoughts, you need to…

2. *Check* your thoughts for evidence, by asking yourself if your thoughts and emotions are solely from today's circumstance/trauma, or are being projected onto today from your past, or a little bit of both. As you check your thoughts, go one level deeper and examine whether how you are thinking is helping or hindering you. If you find your thoughts are largely from past wounds and that your critical needs are currently being met, you can move to…

3. *Change* your fear-based thoughts and replace them with a more positive and truthful narrative.

The more you practice having positive and productive conversations with yourself, the more you fundamentally change your life for the better. The Three C's Technique gives you a practical formula for rewiring your thoughts toward an inner language of love, compassion, patience, and understanding. It helps you develop flexibility of thought. Using the Three C's is a great way to coach yourself back into feeling in control of your emotional reactions and the more impulsive conclusions about any situation.

Healing C-PTSD Through Reparenting

Another effective and practical rewiring solution to navigate your way through emotional triggers is "reparenting"—giving yourself the care and concern you never received from family. You can learn to "healthy-mother" and "healthy-father" yourself. In this example, the focus is on parents. However, all of what you will learn can be applied to siblings and other extended family members who had a negative impact on you growing up. Also, in real life mothers and fathers have a blend of qualities that cross traditional gender stereotypes of "nurturer" and "protector." Still, these are fundamental roles we need our caregivers to play, so in your reparenting I invite you to relate with these basic energies in any form you want to give them, whether you envision them as gendered or genderless, humans or animal spirits, angels, or divine presences.

Healthy Feminine/Mothering Energy

It is instinctive to want and need that compassionate, unconditional love and support of feminine/mothering energy. The mother wound is a painful wound, perhaps the most painful of all. To not have a mother's love is to be void of that soft, warm, secure embrace that makes you feel as if you have a wall of protection around you. Healthy mothering energy is the first to love you, wrap its arms around you, protect you, nurture you, hold your fears, and ease your pain. Your mother is the first person who carves out a special space for your unique purpose in the world. She allows you to understand your true worth. She encourages your determination to be different and to stand out from the rest. She fights for your happiness and gives you the strength to never give up on who you are.

The intention behind healthy mothering is to build that deeply held belief that you are important and deserve to be loved unconditionally. For many survivors, this part of our self-worth was not nurtured or developed.

Moment of Insight: That feeling of "I want my mom" has no age limit, time limit, or distance limit.

Writing in a journal is a great way to mother yourself. When you need someone to talk to, it is a natural instinct to want to talk to your mom. That person who would seemingly never judge you. If your mother was toxic or did not protect you from other abusive family members, she will likely not be the person you turn to. A journal can be an effective substitute. In a journal every part of your inner world has a voice that will be accepted unconditionally, just as it would be if you had a healthy mother. When you write in your journal, you are giving your activated painful emotions the unconditionally caring conversation and nurturing they crave, rather than shaming yourself for having these painful emotions. Writing connects you to your vulnerability and creates the space for your broken pieces to communicate and come together to make better sense of things.

Here are more ways to connect with your inner feminine/mothering energy:

- Surround yourself with wonderful feminine/mothering energy supports.

- Use movement to connect with your body, such as dance, yoga, meditation, or exercise.

- Engage in talk therapy.

- Mother/love your own children, friends, and lovers as they need and deserve.

Healthy Masculine/Fathering Energy

The traits of courage and boldness become important as you go through life. The healthy father/masculine energy is your consummate protector. Whether you had a passive, neglectful, tyrannical, or violent father, you were likely left feeling unprotected, afraid, wary of conflict, or completely nonexistent to the man who was supposed to be your superhero. You can use these skills to correct that relationship within yourself:

- Be the decision maker in your life when it comes to relationship decisions, finances, and career.

- Practice assertiveness by making bold statements of who you are.

- Let the needs you have for yourself be known.

- Channel anger positively into the setting of firm limits.

When you are bold, you learn very quickly who is genuine in your life and who is not. This is a gift. The masculine energy brings clarity—no gossip, no drama, just clarity. This type of clarity helps you to become more discerning and move on from people and situations who cannot and do not support you in being the true, lively, vibrant person you are meant to be.

Healing Affirmations

Affirmations are statements you repeat to yourself—silently, out loud, or in writing—to encourage, affirm, and emotionally support yourself. When you put affirmations on repeat, they assist in rewiring your brain to think in more productive ways. These affirmations, mindsets, and exercises are a worthy practice for healing issues with C-PTSD. The following list of statements/affirmations can help guide and rewire you to be the loving and respectful family member to yourself that you never had.

- I am a good person.

- I am doing my best to always be on my side.

- I do not have to be perfect to get my love and protection.

- All of my feelings are okay with me.

- I am always glad to see myself.

- It is okay to be angry.

- It is okay to make mistakes; it's how I learn.

- I can ask for help, and I will help myself.

- I can have my own preferences and tastes.

- I am a delight to my own eyes.

- I can choose my own values.

- I am very proud of myself.

Take a Moment for You: Reflect on the negative messages you received from your family, verbal or nonverbal, that were counter to the affirming messages in this list. This exercise will bring clarity to what a healthy message from a healthy family member would have looked like, compared to the unhealthy messages you received.

The most important part of rewiring is the firm refusal to indulge in any acts of self-recrimination, self-abandonment, and negative self-talk. *The conversation you have with yourself is the most important and significant of all.* At the end of the day, we each determine our own worth.

Moment of Insight: You must stand against being the victim of how you were raised, while not minimizing that you were victimized.

Patience, compassion, and a positive inner coach make your healing process effective. You can train yourself to get through fears and feelings of panic with less trauma and self-judgment. This allows you to enjoy the journey you are taking into your new life. Best of all, you get to take full credit for putting your life back together. The work you do to heal is work *you* can be proud of. I am certainly proud of you.

How You Can Heal as a Survivor of a Toxic Family

Survivors of toxic family systems need as much information as possible about the reality of their confusing and abusive upbringing. You have been brainwashed and lived with so much uncertainty in areas that were out of your control, that knowing what is in your control will help reestablish feelings of safety. Understanding how and why the loss of your family was, and is, so disorienting and painful is priceless knowledge.

Moment of Insight: You cannot begin to heal your life if you cannot describe what has been done to you.

In my own healing, it was not enough to be an expert on this topic, to know what to expect from my destructive family, to speak about it all over the country, and to continue to live it. I could lie and pretend I am above the hurt my family creates and claim to not give it any power. However, that is simply not true. Whether I like it or not, these people are the family I have, and when they do cruel and spiteful things—whether I have contact with them or not, whether I should expect it or not—it is damaging. When your family members hurt you, you do not hurt as an adult. You hurt as someone's child, someone's daughter, someone's sibling, someone's grand-daughter, someone's niece, someone's parent, or someone's cousin. When others expect you to "be over it" because "you know how your family members are," they inadvertently diminish your experience, past and present. And just like that, your family wound bleeds. Unless you know this is how it works, you cannot cure it. This is why I've explained Erikson's theory of psychosocial development. This information gives you a better idea of when, why, and how your emotional bleeding began and continued to develop as you were maturing.

Healing will also require learning not to mercilessly question yourself over your decision to sever ties. So many of us have gone through a brutal amount of self-interrogation concerning the validity of our experience and our accompanying feelings. It is natural and healthy to question whether what you went through was really bad enough to remove yourself from your family.

It seems that unless your childhood was at the extreme end of abnormal, some others may view the family situation you left as not valid enough to merit severing ties. This adds more pain to your wound. In today's world it is sadly all too normal for children to be pulled through multiple marriages and divorces and to experience traumas like molestation, infidelity, contentious divorce, financial abuse, physical abuse, and addiction destroying the family system. Because these are so common, they're no longer seen as valid reasons to sever ties with family members. If your situation was not overtly abnormal, for example—like that of author Tara Westover, who wrote *Educated* to share her extreme and terrifying story[17]—your abuse can be misperceived, and your cutting ties likely not supported by the larger society. When a parent runs charities or is on the PTA and their abuse is not as overtly obvious, many survivors—me among them—are not supported for taking the exact same steps Tara Westover did to remove ourselves from our family.

Brené Brown, in her book *Braving the Wilderness*, validates the hurt you feel at the hands of family and the social judgments around this topic. She writes:

> Even in the context of suffering—poverty, violence, human rights violations—not belonging in our families is still one of the most dangerous hurts. That's because it has the power to break our heart, our spirit, and our sense of self-worth. And when those things break, there are only three outcomes, something I've borne witness to in my life and in my work: 1. You live in constant pain and seek relief by numbing it and/or inflicting it on others; 2. You deny your pain, and your denial ensures that you pass it on to those around you and down to your children; or 3. You find the courage to own the pain and develop a level of empathy and compassion for yourself and others that allows you to spot hurt in the world in a unique way.[18]

The goal is to get to number three. It may take time and effort to reach this place in your healing. When you think about starting the healing process, it often feels overwhelming. Let me assure you, this is normal. Just because you start the process of your healing does not mean you need to approach a life transformation this profound as if it were a race. You may want to push through your healing as quickly as possible to make your pain stop. Understandable. Unfortunately, there are no short-cuts when dealing with core wounds and their compounding emotional flashbacks. Remember, healing is a verb, always in action. So let's take another step, together, toward healing your emotional loneliness and feelings of disconnection.

Chapter 9

Emotional Loneliness and Feelings of Disconnection

When you enter society estranged from family—and by all accounts your family looks perfect or "normal" from the outside—people falsely assume your family is a good one and your decision to cut ties is wrong. Sadly, it is easier in many ways for survivors if there are obvious reasons, such as addiction or mental illness, because the acceptance and support you so desperately need comes more naturally and wholeheartedly. It is hard to understand or validate unspoken abuses that are not obvious or clear to others. You have no words or hard evidence that seem to prove what is hidden. Without this overt evidence of your psychological abuse, you experience loneliness and isolation from two different sources: family and society. But there are many toxic mothers, fathers, siblings, and so on who appear community minded—apparently generous in their service, time, charity, and altruism out in their social world—who turn into a "home devil" in the private realm of family.

> **Take a Moment for You:** Reflect on how many years you justified abuse because you were not sure if your abuse was "real enough."

When you grow up feeling cast out, alienated, controlled, criticized, used, and overtly picked on, that is abuse and emotional abandonment in tandem. This treatment is bad enough for you to set definitive boundaries. Ultimately, there is no way to leave a toxic family or stay in one without feeling abandoned. Abandonment doesn't always mean being left in a basket on someone's doorstep, never to see your family members again. Abandonment comes from a feeling of not belonging; that you are in the way, an annoyance, or not valid enough as a person to be worthy of another's time, love, and attention.

One clue to help you know where or when you need to pause and tend to your wounds is when you are experiencing deep levels of loneliness and feelings of disconnection without just cause in your adult relationships.

> *Elissa is a client who struggles with feeling abandoned, even when she is not being abandoned. Elissa will be cuddling on the couch with her boyfriend but have the sense they are not connecting. She states that "he feels far away" because he's winding down and a little quiet after a long day at work. Her boyfriend's being quiet makes her feel agitated. When she confronts him, her boyfriend gets frustrated because he cannot understand how or why she feels this way, when he feels they are connecting and simply enjoying the evening together. He says, "It's not like I am so quiet that we aren't talking at all, so I don't understand. She makes me feel like I am constantly letting her down."*

Elissa grew up with emotionally unavailable parents. She needs a level of reassurance, attention, and validation that she has been unable to satisfy in her relationships. These types of issues are a sign that your significant relationships in childhood were not supportive or nurturing. Like Elissa, you need to learn to fill the hole in your heart with your own healing; otherwise, no matter how much love, attention, or reassurance you receive from another, you will always feel let down.

The Abandonment Wound

A remarkable book by Susan Anderson, *The Journey from Abandonment to Healing*,[19] details the intensity of emotional abandonment and the grief that takes place over the course of a lifetime when trying to recover from it. There is a huge difference between the grief of abandonment and the grief that comes after a death. When a person in your life passes away, they are not passing away to damage or spite you (with the possible exception of suicide, which is outside the scope of the topic here). When someone passes away through illness, accident, violence, or old age, it is a natural part of life; it is not their fault, and it is not your fault. In other words, you do not cause their natural death with your less-than-desirable human flaws.

With emotional abandonment, on the other hand, you are losing someone you deeply love and feel you need, knowing this person is choosing not to be with you, not to keep you in their life. This type of rejection is enough to leave you reeling in indescribable grief and despair. When someone you love chooses not to be with you, you do not just lose the relationship with that person; you also lose a core belief in yourself as significant and worthy.

Anderson states that abandonment grief is a syndrome of its own. What gives abandonment grief its particular flavor is the way in which you turn fear and anger against yourself. This tendency toward self-attack makes abandonment grief profoundly different from grief for a death. Abandonment survivors are sensitive, caring, and ready for love, and for some of you, abandonment grief can be so long-lasting that it stands in the way of your finding and sustaining love.[20] The abandonment wound leaves you questioning whether you are lovable or acceptable in love and relationships. This invisible or imagined personal defect is the starting point of your feelings of self-hate. And so you bleed.

Self-Love Starts with Examining Self-Hate

The main cause of self-hate is trauma, which includes but is not limited to sexual, physical, or emotional abuse, abandonment, or neglect. To feel abandoned awakens a primal fear that you will be left alone forever with no one to protect you or to witness your most urgent needs. Out of this fear arises an intense anger. You are angry for having to feel so much anxiety, loneliness, and desperation. You feel dumbfounded as to why you are powerless to hold on to another person's love.

These feelings of helplessness drive deep levels of self-hate. Because your toxic family members love only with conditions, it is easy to see how you learned the habit of becoming preoccupied with self-hate, beating yourself up, focusing solely on your flaws and foibles, and, at worst, rationalizing and justifying your abandonment. You have effectively turned against yourself. You live believing you have some horrible defect in your character, but totally confused as to what this defect is. Yet each time you experience fear of abandonment, it is easy to fall into this warped belief you are somehow too fatally flawed to be loved.

> **Moment of Insight:** When you are constantly criticized by your family, you do not stop loving them. You stop loving yourself.

Your feelings of emotional exile after having been abandoned can be so strong they blind you to your abuse. Instead, these feelings make you yearn for and obsessively crave the family members who have emotionally deserted you. You erroneously believe if your family could just love you, your life would be peaceful. Sadly, your family counts on your obsessive yearning for them, because it keeps you in the position of the underling, with you constantly seeking and needing their approval. This yearning ensures that you will unconsciously continue to allow your family to manipulate you, because even as an adult you will continue to endlessly try to repair relationships with your family members by doing your absolute best to be "good" in their eyes.

> **Moment of Insight:** The irony is, your toxic family members expect you to be perfect, even when they have been far from model parents, siblings, grandparents, and so on.

Because abandonment is so devastating, it is a feeling or experience you would never want to inflict on another person. So it is that sadly, many survivors hold back from making this crucial decision—which would benefit their own mental health—for fear that they are abandoning their family when they cut ties. Remember, there is a big difference between setting boundaries on the abuse and abandonment you feel every day and cutting someone off because you're having an angry moment.

Have You Abandoned Your Family?

When you sever ties with a toxic family, you are *not* abandoning them. You are establishing no contact so that *they* can no longer abandon *you*. Your toxic family members are experts at emotional abandonment. They can dodge the pangs of guilt and awareness of the cruelty of their actions by choosing to remain oblivious to the negative impact of their treatment. They numb themselves to the damage they cause through their actions by viewing it as justifiable. They simply lack compassion. They don't value or care about truth. This numbing defense allows your family to maintain an image of themselves as decent, caring human beings. Their rigid denial of their abuse and manipulation comes across as callous to those of you who are left to pick up the pieces. Ironically, you may still feel abandoned even after having removed yourself from your abusers, because each day that your family places being right over the relationship they could have with you is another day added to your abandonment.

> **Moment of Insight:** Survivors of family abuse live life with the heart of an orphan.

For many survivors, abandonment wounds may not fully heal, but rather lurk beneath the surface of their self-belief throughout adulthood. This is especially true when you are surrounded by reminders of family when spending time around others and their families. It is easy to become triggered when you see the healthy parents of people you know who are helpful and selfless with their children, or when you witness them and their siblings, cousins, and other extended family showing they genuinely love each other and have each other's best interests at heart. These triggers remind you of what you never had.

Luckily, abandonment wounds are not hopeless. Here are some effective healing skills to try:

- *Write a letter to the person/people who abandoned you, then burn it.* This ceremonial approach helps you release your desires to connect and be understood. If you cannot find this in your family, give it to the universe.

- *Write a supportive, caring letter to the vulnerable emotions of longing you experience.* Letter writing to your vulnerable emotions is a great way to soothe them and to practice positive self-talk.

- *Allow yourself to feel the gamut of emotions attached to your aban-donment.* In toxic families you are not allowed to speak out loud what is going on inside you without being punished and having your words twisted. Feel what you need to feel.

- *Identify the part of you that feels hurt, such as your inner child.* Examine whatever part of you is hurting, and give this part of you love and compassion.

- *View your inner child as healthy, strong, and capable.* Create a vision for your inner child as being an inner badass. That inner child of yours has survived a tremendous amount and deserves to be acknowledged for its strength and perseverance.

- *List the coping mechanisms you can count on to help you manage your thoughts and emotions.* List making is hugely powerful. It helps bring objectivity to the table, along with a sense of hope and new ideas for your future.

- *Talk to and soothe your hurt places by reassuring your panicked emo-tions.* Being soothed and reassured is fundamental to healing. Make sure you're doing this for yourself whenever you need it.

As you embark on healing the wounds of abandonment and rejection, the concept of wanting to feel validated will likely surface. It's normal and natural to need and want your painful experiences to be validated. Coming from deep family dysfunction, either consciously or subconsciously you likely carry the need for someone, *anyone*, to step in and give you the feeling that there is a protective shield over you.

Take a Moment for You: How has your pain not been validated by the family members who caused it? How has this lack of valida-tion affected you?

When we survivors, myself included, are emotionally triggered, what many of the significant people in our life don't see is our need for them to meet us in the emotional state we are experiencing, with the same tender-ness and softness they would offer a child. Keep in mind that when you are hurting, the "adult resumé" of your accomplishments does not matter. What matters is compassion. You need to have your experiences heard and taken seriously. Support from others breeds understanding and connection. It generates trust. It creates a sacred and safe place for you to tell the truth of your story without worrying that you will be cast out. This sounds easy, yet so many survivors struggle to find themselves in healthy and supportive relationships as adults.

Establishing Emotionally Validating Relationships

It is common for survivors to attract relationships with people who avoid emotional intimacy and are inconsistent in their lovingness. This attraction to emotionally unavailable people keeps you stuck in your dysfunctional familial pattern that triggers your painful feelings about love—the feeling that love is not there for you. Survivors desire, more than anything, to be in emotionally satisfying relationships that substantiate and uphold them. So why are these so challenging to find? Here are some reasons:

- *You have suffered family abuse.* It is natural to carry the pain of your childhood by unconsciously seeking relationships with people similar to those who raised you. The chaos you suffered under is the unhealthy version of attachment you are drawn to because it is emotionally charged. These highly charged emotions are intoxicating, as is the desire to resolve them. It is this intoxication that keeps you hooked.

- *You are honest and feel hurt when questioned.* Growing up under constant criticism and twisted versions of reality causes you to suffer from deep levels of self-doubt and anxiety about whether others will accept, embrace, and believe your opinions, feelings, and ideas. Because of these fears, you too often give your power away by trying to get people to trust your version of events.

- *You believe that love comes only from achievement.* Many of us learned that love had to be earned and was rationed based on performance. We unconsciously apply this dysfunctional formula to our adult attachments. We tend to pick people who allow us to carry the load of the work and who will also blame us when we resent having to do so.

- *You tend to be perfectionistic.* Never feeling you have achieved enough or are enough can cause you to over-function. Over-functioning signals to other people that they can use you. All it takes is for someone to make you feel imperfect, and you reflexively jump into action. There's a saying: *Perfection is trauma all dressed up.*

- *You're prone to wanting to fix other people's problems.* Toxic family systems are built in reverse. Toxic parents, siblings, uncles, aunts, and grandparents see no issue with putting undue stress and problems onto their children and/or other family members. This habit of taking care of your family easily turns into a chronic pattern of being the caretaker or fixer.

- *You have challenges with assertiveness and setting boundaries.* In psychologically abusive families, asserting yourself is not an option. At any moment of trying to stand up for yourself, your efforts were more than likely ignored, gaslighted, or punished. So you enter relationships with fears of criticism, rejection, abandonment, and punishment (CRAP). Because of this CRAP, you fear setting boundaries.

- *You avoid situations that threaten abandonment.* Because you were raised to fear being discarded, this provokes your need to do anything and everything to avoid abandonment, even to the extent of sacrificing what is best for you. This drives you into codependent relationships. You are so afraid of being rejected that you learn to prefer a false sense of security to true love.

Take a Moment for You: Reflect on these underlying reasons for picking less-than-satisfying relationships as an adult, and consider how you can make changes in these areas. You deserve healthy, happy relationships that will validate you as an important, significant, and lovable person. When you are never acknowledged, it is hard to feel worthy.

All this is part of the patterns of invalidation. Invalidation happens when the person you love denies, minimizes, criticizes, or ignores your emotional experiences, ideas, feelings, hurts, communication, or opinions. It is incredibly painful to feel that those you love are not hearing you or are misunderstanding you, diminishing your experience, or ignoring what you need. It is okay to have needs. However, needing repeated, ongoing reassurance from others is also unhealthy and often sets you up for the abandonment you are trying to avoid because it makes you seem needy. Neediness is one of the leading relationship killers.

When you are needy, you push people way. Neediness presents itself through insecurity—nagging, never feeling happy, making chronic quests for reassurance, and making it impossible for another to satisfy you emotionally. As you heal, you want more than anything to keep the people you love in your life. To do that, you must work to heal your issues around neediness. You greatly increase your chances to find yourself in emotionally satisfying relationships when you learn to validate, reassure, and provide for yourself. Here are ways you can validate yourself:

- Acknowledge your strengths, successes, progress, and effort.

- Accept your internal experience: your thoughts, feelings, and emotional states.

- Identify the triggers that make you feel invalidated.

- Prioritize your needs and, as much as possible, meet them yourself.

- Treat yourself with kindness.

- Use positive self-talk.

- Accept your limitations, flaws, and mistakes; you are human.

- Do not compare yourself to others.

- Pay attention to how you feel and what you need.

- Accept yourself without judgment.

- Treat yourself like a friend.

- Give yourself the love you never got.

Moment of Insight: You will only grow apart from people who don't grow.

When the bandwidth of your tolerance for the immature, game-playing dynamics of your family is finally used up, you are left feeling frustrated and alone. Feelings of loneliness provoke many survivors to start looking, consciously or unconsciously, for a replacement family to fill their void. This is normal and natural, but not always a healthy way to fix what is broken. No one person, no matter how wonderful, can erase or undo the wounds left by your family. When you fully accept your unfortunate circumstances, it helps you become less needy for anyone outside of you to heal or replace what could have or should have been for you. You grow to acknowledge that you have a family, and you grow to accept that your family has failed you, even when that acceptance feels like swallowing sand. There is a limited bandwidth to hope, and toxic family systems will use yours up. With acceptance, your hope can turn toward the promise of healing yourself.

Chapter 10

Emerge from Feeling Broken

When you are young, it is easier to believe that you are not lovable than it is to believe that your family members aren't capable of loving you. This leads to a feeling of being broken somehow. However, this feeling does not mean you are not loved or that you are not a lovable person. You simply are not loved by a family who is lovable or capable of love. To emerge from feeling broken will require you to accept this.

You have a family, they are poisonous, and no other person or family can heal wounds in you that they didn't inflict. Only your own family would have the potential to do that, and they won't. Good news: Acceptance of this reality will eventually bring reprieve. For me personally, it is a relief to no longer look at my phone and see a name coming in on caller ID that raises my blood pressure. However, accepting my reality was also excruciating at first. After years of pain, I finally came to recognize that there wasn't an available healthy relationship in my family that was worth fighting for. Healthy relationships simply did not and still do not exist in that dynamic.

The process of acceptance clears the confusion you were raised in that turned you against yourself. With distance between yourself and your family, you become clear that you were not the truly broken person; rather, that description fits your destructive family members. It is quite liberating to embrace the realization that living well does not require a close-knit family (although you may want one), and therefore you can heal yourself in order to forge healthy bonds of your own making.

Moment of Insight: You do not treat people the way you have been treated by your family members and call it love.

The loss of your True Self never should have been a requirement to secure love from your family. As you emerge from feeling broken and work your way toward living your life wholeheartedly, you will slowly start to feel the joy of what it is like to be exactly who you are, without fear.

The Value of a Therapeutic Relationship

You can become the loving presence in your life that you've never had before. It will require self-awareness and a commitment to learning and embracing self-love. I am a psychologist by trade and education, so I certainly believe in the value of self-examination. I also do not believe I am above the healing process simply because I am a psychologist. I take pride in being a therapist who sees a therapist. In my own therapeutic journey, I am provided the space to do the continual work of mourning the family I wish I had had, and to cope with the societal judgments I face in having severed ties with them. Because most of my family members are still alive, I cannot fully grieve them. In therapy I have the space to be honest when I am feeling pure revulsion for my family members and their antics. When I feel the need to love them and I run into their stubborn, petulant refusal to love and accept me, my loving feelings for my family transmute into feelings of frustration, resignation, and disappointment. These are the authentic feelings and experiences survivors can openly express without judgment in the therapy relationship, where cutting ties does not need to be a taboo act—one that, despite being widespread, must be kept silent.

Therapy is a safe place to be completely shameless. It is a place to receive the feedback and support you need that will help you develop the courage and insight to feel better and live better. Therapy protects you from lapsing back into the illusion that somewhere or somehow your toxic family members could one day be the people you so urgently needed and still need—those empathic, open, understanding, understandable, honest, available, helpful, loving, feeling, supportive, transparent, clear, and uncontradictory family members. Such family members were never yours to begin with.

The therapy relationship provides you with the consistency, predictability, and nurturing you never received in the first stage of your life when it was vital to develop the virtues of trust and hope. It is a relationship that supports you to be both vulnerable and brave. I do not always have a lot to talk about at the start of some sessions, as is also true for many of my own patients, but I benefit just as greatly from therapy on these days by simply being in the presence of a healthy, honest, and nurturing relationship. It is the cumulative impact of the consistency and stability of the therapeutic relationship (that your family should have provided), rather than the detail of any individual session, that is so profoundly healing and transformational.

Take a Moment for You: Reflect on how you think a therapeutic relationship could benefit you.

Resurrecting Your Broken Places

Before you can emerge from feeling broken, you must resurrect and awaken your broken places in order to learn from them. Whatever you have hidden away from your conscious view may wreak havoc in your life. Taking on any type of self-examination endeavor, you must apply the wisdom of patience to your healing. Healing yourself will not be a one-time event where you fully recover your broken places over a weekend seminar, but a lifelong process that will take your long-term focus and commitment.

Moment of Insight: Be brave enough to face your broken places, even when it hurts.

It will not be hard to locate your damaged places when you find yourself facing the consistent scrutiny of the larger society over your decision to cut ties, in combination with your feelings of being alone.

As unfortunate and unfair as this is, because you have cut ties, many people in society will hold you accountable for creating your own pain. They project onto you that you are not allowed to hurt, since you were the person who severed ties. Living with these two realities means you will constantly feel as if you have to retrieve your heart from the lost and found. This happens because you are stuck between your decision and much of the larger social world pushing back on what you need. This leaves you feeling "found" in your own decision to sever ties but "lost" when trying to find support and acceptance. Many fail to grasp that once you have arrived at the decision to sever ties with family, you have learned the hard way that you cannot heal by trying to change anyone else, nor can you heal while waiting and hoping that one day your family members will change.

The one place and person you have any influence over is yourself. The most powerful thing to recognize is that each of us is the starting place for our own transformation. Your transformation is no longer about waiting for your family to change or waiting for society to accept your decision.

For you to transform your life, it is most helpful to start with an examination of the limiting beliefs about who you are that were programmed into you.

The Negative Influence of Limiting Beliefs

Limiting beliefs are the false beliefs you hold about yourself that have a deeply negative impact on your life. Believing poor things about yourself places restraints of fear and inhibition around what you will or will not do, say, or be. With limiting beliefs, you leave childhood compromised with emotional triggers in the following areas:

Self-Acceptance

You grow up with the erroneous belief that you are not enough. You must learn to stop this pervasive feeling by interrupting its path.

Take a Moment for You: Reflect on how and why you may believe you are not enough. How can you learn to disrupt that thought pattern and remind yourself that you may not be perfect, but you are good enough?

Clear Sense of Identity

Psychologically abusive families raise you to be what you think others want you to be. The problem with codependency is it places you in a relationship with yourself based in chronic neglect. Because you never found acceptance in your family system, you likely battle with intense and persistent worry over whether you are doing the right thing, in the correct way, and whether you could or should be doing anything differently or better for everyone but yourself.

> **Take a Moment for You:** Reflect that healing comes when you drop the idea that you must "fit" somewhere or with a specific group of people.

Self-Compassion

Because you were raised in a compassionless environment, you never learned that you were worthy of compassion. Lack of self-compassion is one of the key factors that leads you to choose the wrong people to love in adulthood.

> **Take a Moment for You:** Reflect on how you feel inside when you consider putting your own needs first. Do you feel shameful, guilty, selfish, afraid?

Anger and Rage

Destructive family systems raise you to believe that if you get angry, you are bad. This is when they will start calling you mentally ill and/or out of control. In reality, anger is a healthy emotion until it gets repressed. When anger is repressed, it turns to rage. It is common for survivors to report that their family members have the power to get them to rage unlike anyone else in their life has ever been able to. Why? Because in toxic families you have to repress everything you feel. Eventually, when constantly provoked, what is repressed boils over. This makes sense. Anger arises out of the need to set boundaries. Rage comes when the boundaries are perpetually disrespected. Anger lets you know when you have had enough. It shows up to help you confront and establish your nonnegotiables. The better you protect yourself, the more others will grow to respect you, and the less anger you will carry. *Anger is the one emotion with the potential to create change, because it is the one emotion that leads you to bring justice to an injustice.*

Take a Moment for You: Reflect on how you can trust your anger. How can you make your anger serve you rather than hurt you?

Capacity to Draw Comfort from Relationships

Because a loving environment was not your norm, you can expect you may struggle to feel "comfort" in relationships. Speaking from my own personal experience, I can draw love from relationships, but I struggle greatly to draw comfort from them; to trust their sustainability. Relationships have been more anxiety producing than peaceful in my life. When I am in love, I struggle to trust the stability and/or intentions of others enough to give myself fully. I am the girl who always has a plan B.

Catastrophizing is an old habit that dies hard, because, perhaps like you, I have been trained to expect the worst from people and get the worst. To heal this issue is a tough one. It may or may not be possible for you to draw comfort from relationships, depending on the extent of your issues with trust and abandonment. The good news is, it is likely that you can draw love from relationships, if not comfort. Here is what I have learned: *The more deeply and authentically you live your own life, and the more connected you are to your own individual purpose outside of your love relationships, the more comfort you will feel in the relationship you have with yourself.* The more comfortable you become with who you are, the more comfort you will feel when with others.

Take a Moment for You: Reflect on whether you can draw comfort from relationships. How can you work to expand that capacity?

Ability to Relax

You were raised to believe you were never doing enough. From this feeling, you commit to being busy and staying in action to prove you are endlessly *trying* to be better. You do this to gain the perpetually elusive approval you have always longed for from your family. Yet this type of busyness also serves as a distraction from your trauma. Relaxing likely feels uncomfortable, maybe even selfish. When you relax it can bring up feelings of worthlessness. If you're not rushed, cleaning, overworked, overachieving, or doing something to make life perfect, you may feel as if you cease to exist in any meaningful way.

> **Take a Moment for You:** Reflect on how it may be helpful for you to accept that no matter how much you distract yourself with busyness, it will not make your trauma go away. What then?

Capacity for Self-Expression

In toxic family environments, it is better to be seen but not heard. This makes knowing how or when to express yourself confusing and challenging. It was overtly or covertly demanded that you accept your circumstances and go with the flow of the dysfunction. This made it clear your needs and opinions had zero influence to effect change in your family life. To avoid this pain, many of us reflexively learned to shut down our emotions to achieve some level of acceptance.

> **Take a Moment for You:** Reflect on the idea that to heal you must resurrect the spirit of your own voice. How can you do this?

Discipline and Motivation

When raised in a family where nothing you do is acknowledged as worthy, it is easy to lose motivation to do anything. Some of you may use a lack of motivation to rebel against the nagging and unrealistic pressures placed on you by family as a way to assert control over your life.

> **Take a Moment for You:** Reflect on this question: How have you been dealing with discipline or motivation?

Ability to Self-Care

The concepts of "care" and "concern" in destructive family systems flow in one direction: the more sensitive, vulnerable person has to make sure the toxic person in the relationship is catered to. This type of systematic coercion does not effectively meet the needs of all involved. You were raised to see no value in caring for yourself. The only time you were seen as valuable was when you were the emotional slave or janitor to your family members.

Take a Moment for You: Reflect on self-care. Do you give yourself permission to do this?

Seeing Life as a Gift

Far from seeing life as a gift, you grew up experiencing life as painful, scary, tricky, twisted, and unpredictable. The goal of a toxic family is to keep you down so you will not develop the confidence necessary to separate from the control they have established over you. When you are not the leader of your life, it is nearly impossible to experience life as a gift.

Take a Moment for You: Reflect on your thoughts about life. Do you see life as a gift?

As you work with negative beliefs about yourself, others, and life in general, it can feel painful, because to counter negative beliefs you must fully see them. Become honest with yourself, every day, one day at a time, and the day will come when you will tell the story of how you overcame what you went through, and it will become someone else's survival guide. If you can learn to trust yourself, trust what your trauma responses communicate about what isn't and wasn't right, and trust the emotional triggers that arise as opportunities for healing, you will have gained a life of emotional freedom.

Fundamentally Trust Yourself

Human beings are hardwired to love and attach, specifically with those individuals who make up our tribe. How can you grow if you cannot connect with others? Without tangible human connection, your growth would be extremely shallow. Unfortunately, connection and manipulation cannot healthfully coexist.

When it comes to establishing healthy connections, the virtue of trust will prove to be more valuable than love, because you cannot safely love someone you cannot trust. Manipulation is set directly against the establishment of trust, so your desire for connection comes more from fear than from love. When you attach based on fear, you are attaching based on trauma, not trust. Your trauma does bear great gifts, however, because your trauma is the portal to your most wounded places. Without this portal, healing wouldn't be possible. This portal opens when you are emotionally triggered.

Moment of Insight: When you have self-respect, your compulsion toward peace becomes stronger than any addiction to chaos you learned to have.

Your trauma sets off emotional warnings inside your emotional system. An emotional trigger is something that ignites a memory tape in your mind that transports you back to the feelings of the original wound. Emotional triggers are personal. Different things trigger different people. However, triggers tend to present themselves in the following areas: feeling misunderstood, unsupported, ostracized, criticized; feeling not thought of or not taken seriously; not trusting oneself; feeling let down, uncertain, unattractive, not smart, stressed, abandoned, not credible; feeling afraid of conflict, or being humiliated or taken advantage of; feeling vulnerable; and when anticipating unexpected change. Unexamined emotional triggers block the establishment of the type of trust required for intimacy and connection, so you must learn to work with them, rather than against them.

Emotional Triggers as Portals for Transformation

When used correctly, emotional triggers act as gateways with the potential to illuminate to you where you need to establish your limits and boundaries. Note that emotional triggers do not mature as you age, because human beings reflexively regress under stress. Because your triggers do not age, you will naturally respond to current stressors from an emotionally regressed place. It does not mean your feelings are not valid in the current moment, but they may be more wounded than the current stressor calls for. This is why understanding and identifying the situations that trigger you is a giant step in your growth.

You will undoubtedly fall down the rabbit hole of emotional triggers, because people are going to accidentally say and do things that aggravate your wounds, and before you know it, you find yourself feeling overwhelmed with insecurity or defensiveness. To cope with this, I suggest you use time as an ally to help modulate your emotions. Emotions compel you to act. However, when emotions are running high, you can rely only on the truth of any situation you are in. Taking time to process what's happening gives you the space to move your thoughts and emotions from reactivity toward rationality. Emotional maturity comes from engaging these four steps when you've been triggered:

1. Identify the trigger to the family wound.

2. Sit with and feel the emotions provoked by the trigger (fear, abandonment, anger, and so on) without acting on them.

3. Identify what type of help or support may be necessary to establish clarity before deciding to take action or not (therapy, journaling, meditation, exercise, worship, talking to a trusted friend).

4. Examine where the old wound intersects with the current trigger to avoid projecting stronger emotions than necessary onto the current situation.

The benefit of going through this type of process is to slow down your thoughts, emotions, and most importantly your desire to take impulsive action. This process helps you to live with poise. Giving yourself a minute to digest your feelings and thoughts often leads you to the understanding that the person or situation that has currently hurt you was not intentionally trying to dig at your old wounds. Because of the abuse and manipulation you were raised in, you may unknowingly feel or assume others may be acting in a purposefully harmful manner toward you, because this is all you know. This faulty belief can cause you to end relationships that do not need to end. Perhaps all that is needed is a little work, patience, and communication.

It is understandable you may have to fight the urge to leave a relationship when someone hurts you. However, no-contact boundaries should not be used just because you are having a toxic or confusing moment in a relationship. Is this murky? Absolutely. Yet this is not a habit that will lead to happiness, nor will it help you create lasting or trusted relationships. Learning to be a good governor of your emotions will help you become a better communicator and a better nurturer of yourself and others.

When you learn to be present for yourself in times of need, you equip yourself to be present and transparent in your most meaningful relationships. This is how you can heal your broken places. When you take care of yourself first, everything else falls more naturally into place. Taking care of yourself leads you toward self-compassion and self-love.

Chapter 11

Moving Toward Empathy and Self-Love

As you know, toxic people have no desire to go under the microscope of self-examination, and therefore they are unable to feel empathy for other people or give any credence to another person's perspective. They view themselves as above censure. When you have been raised by those who show no empathy, you go through many years of picking friends and partners who lack empathy as well. This is all part of your healing journey. You must keep in mind, however, that no relationship is a mistake unless you waste your pain by choosing to learn nothing from it. Make use of your mistakes by learning about empathy and its restorative impact on your personal development.

Empathy is your awareness of other people's feelings and emotions. You place yourself in another's shoes, to feel what they feel as deeply as if their situation were happening to you. Empathy is a critical element of *emotional intelligence*, which consists of measurable—and growable—skills for relating to emotions, whether your own or those of others. Empathy bonds you to others in deep emotional connections. This goes far beyond sympathy, which you can think of as feeling *for* someone. Empathy is feeling *with* that person, using assumption and imagination. Empathy is gained through your more painful life moments; developed through rejection, heartbreak, hurt, failure, and feeling humiliated or ashamed; and through allowing yourself to be seen. In essence, your own history of pain helps you perceive, and relate with, the pain others feel.

One of the most powerful and useful tools to establish empathetic and meaningful connections with others is the telling of your story. Your story is powerful enough to make others feel as if they are not alone; that there are others who have suffered as they have or are currently suffering. Your personal story is full of emotion and experience. Emotions are the universal language common to all, which is why they have such a great potential to bond us with others. Your story makes you real, it makes you human, it makes you relatable, and it defines who you are and how you came to be this person. So telling your story builds bonds and creates a community for survivors based in empathy and relatability.

The Curative Gifts of Telling Your Story

It is natural to desire sharing your story of overcoming and to want others to be receptive to what your story tells them about who you are. The most powerful thing you do in this life is telling your story. In telling my story in my first book, *Loving Yourself: The Mastery of Being Your Own Person*, I was looking to have my pain openly seen by my family, to feel cared for by them, to feel they were remorseful, and to feel the empathy from them I had never received. I desperately needed to feel that the truth of my experience mattered to them, to hear that they were genuinely sorry, and that in some way they were doing their best with what they had or knew. Typical of any toxic person, my family did not see my book as *my* story, but rather as a story about *them*. If they were to read my subsequent books, they would feel the same way and continue to gaslight my experience. They would call me a liar. Yet I could not make this stuff up if I tried.

In sharing my story, I learned that the truth of your family situation will not alter, no matter how your family members try and subtract from it, excuse it, gaslight it, or lie to cover it up. None of these antics make the truth any less than or any different from what the truth already is. You have no responsibility to negotiate a truth that is not negotiable. This is why so many patients and other people who have lived this abusive family dynamic feel tremendous relief that I understand them—not from what I have studied, but from what I have suffered that is so eerily similar to what they have suffered.

Moment of Insight: Never sacrifice your truth to a system of lies.

I no longer hold any hope that my story could help, enlighten, assist, or change my family. Understanding this has been liberation in the truest and deepest sense, and also my sole/soul objective for you. The books I am writing today are for *you*. The intention is to have *you* use them to connect with yourself and to similar others in a shared experience where empathy and understanding are available and abundant. I want you and your story to have a place, so you no longer suffer in silence. Here are some ways you can tell your story:

- In writing, whether you share it or not. A journal is a safe place in which to be fully expressed. It's a private place to express reactive thoughts and to find the wisdom in your pain before you share it directly with another. If you don't journal, you can write in letter form directly to your abuser, or you can simply take notes on a pad of paper or on your phone.

- In therapy. The therapy relationship is designed to be a safe, contained environment for you to empty your emotional baggage without judgment. In it, you will be encouraged to find the meaning in your suffering to empower your overall potential as a human being.

- With a trusted friend or loved one. Friends can be as good as a therapist if they are able to hold a safe, nonjudgmental space for you to express yourself.

Moment of Insight: The more you tell your story and the more it is seen, heard, and validated by others, the more you heal and the more deeply you can connect with others from a place of mutual understanding and empathy.

There's a tricky thing about empathy. You may have learned the hard way that being empathetic can be both a blessing and a curse. To feel *with* another is an incredible blessing. It creates the space for each person to be fully accepted in the rawness of their vulnerabilities. Empathy lets you know that you are not alone and that you will be okay. However, empathy can be a curse when you unknowingly empathize with a toxic person who uses your soft-hearted nature to further exploit and manipulate you, thereby driving you into deeper and deeper levels of insecurity.

The silver lining of being empathetic is that you can develop a healthy refusal to spend even one minute of your life around anyone who is toxic for you. When you too quickly assume good in another, it can be deadly. You need to learn to be an empathetic person within a protective shield. This way, you don't operate solely from love or wishful thinking, but rather from a place of being grounded in your observed reality.

The Educated Empath

Being an educated empath means you use the wisdom gleaned from past heartbreaks to decide who you will allow into your life and who you will not. This means you pay attention to a person's actions rather than their words. Manipulators are word magicians. Their words often sound wonderful and promise many things, but what they say is very rarely reflected in their actions. The words they use do nothing more than twist your mind. You want to be in touch with your reality, not with what you *want* your reality to be. Reality clears away false hope and saves you from getting stuck in "potential." When you operate from an empathetic intelligence, you do not use defenses like denial, justification, pleasing, or choosing comfort over courage. You operate from maturity, objectivity, discernment, grace, and awareness.

Right or wrong, it is my belief that empaths should be in therapy. Life is intense for you. You see things. You feel things. You know things. Sometimes these things hurt, but you must also embrace that everything that hurts also has the potential to heal. To protect your exposed heart, you can come to follow your intuition and trust what you know. Therapy will help you stop the habit of turning red-flag warnings about people into lighter shades of pink through twisted justifications and fears. It will help you possess the wisdom and insight to never justify manipulation of any kind. Therefore you must refuse to allow others to determine, control, or sway you away from the truth you hold deep inside.

Here are ways to become an educated empath:

- Set firm boundaries around anyone who has treated you poorly without cause.

- Have a no-tolerance policy toward anyone who dismisses your reality based on accusations of being too sensitive or who accuses you of having "excessive" boundaries.

- Commit to being in mutually satisfying relationships, ending those that are not.

- Trust deeply in your instincts to know who is toxic and who is not.

- Refuse to waste time and energy explaining decisions to those who refuse to understand.

- Use silence as a superpower. When there is nothing nice to say, it is better to say nothing at all.

Yes, it's true that being an empath makes you a better friend, a better lover, and a better and more available parent. However, you will not become capable of helping or healing others if you cannot first help and heal yourself. Family scapegoats are earth angels. You are not the burden you have been told you are. You are here, in this life, for a very special purpose. You possess the natural gift of empathy for a reason. See your empathetic nature for the precious and life-affirming gift that it is.

The Power of Self-Love

Miracles happen when you start focusing on nourishing and investing in yourself. Try using empathy in place of being self-critical when seeking to accomplish self-love. When you have self-love, you accept without shame or self-abuse that there are things for you to learn, that life will give you the exact experiences you need to evolve, that the person you struggle to trust the most is yourself, and that your family members didn't betray you so much as they revealed to you the truth of who they are. When you look at pain from this vantage point, it is healing.

Your path into self-love is a venture toward recovery and discovery. It is a place of new mindsets and looking at your family from a more expansive perspective, instead of from the narrow version of them they want you to see. Self-love is about expansion, not contraction. The greatest thing about love is that love is always within you. There are no limits to the love you can grow inside of yourself.

> **Moment of Insight:** You must choose yourself, even when others refuse to.

To get to this place, examine the relationship patterns around "love" that you were raised in, and ascertain how they impact your vision of what love should look like today. Remember, you learned to love yourself by modeling how your family members loved you. If love wasn't present then, it makes sense you would not know how to love yourself. Take a look at these patterns of love within your life and heart:

- When you think about loving yourself, what childhood patterns do you recognize for how love was expressed or not expressed in your family?

- Can you identify themes from your family that are now reflected in your adult relationships?

- Was the love you received healthy, abundant, respectful, consistent, and noninvasive?

- What about the love you saw your parents or other family members share with each other? Were there favorites and outcasts?

When you do this kind of inquiry, you can start loving yourself in the ways you were never loved. Here are effective ways to love yourself:

- Allow yourself to feel all your emotions.

- Stop behaving as if you are "less than" to protect someone else's ego.

- Do not allow the love you have for someone to make you ignore the toxic truth about them, or you will hurt yourself in the process.

- Allow yourself to be authentic, honest, and true.

- When you are hurting, remember that diamonds are made under the weight of mountains. There will be growth.

- Give up the need for approval from every single person in your life.

- Sacrifice a little bit of your present for your future. Work out when you do not feel like it, instead of scrolling on your phone for an hour. Always do what is good for your future self.

Even keeping these self-love methods in mind will open up the possibility that you will want to care for yourself. As you heal, you'll begin to find your value and open to a new experience of love by offering it to yourself. Now that you want wholeness and wellness for yourself, there are things you can do to create it.

Importance of Self-Care

Self-care defines the actions you take to reach optimal levels of physical, emotional, mental, relational, and spiritual wellness. Coming from dysfunction, you have spent a tremendous amount of time ardently believing that if you could just find the right words, the clearest examples or illustrations, with the right intensity, delivered at the right time, with the perfect tone of voice, with all the correct facts and evidence to prove your abuse, you could bring about understanding and connection between yourself and your family members. This has not been and will not be a winning formula for you.

Moment of Insight: Overexplaining is a trauma response.

You need to hear professionals, and those who love you, say that it is a valiant act of self-care to walk away from the abuses of your family whenever you are ready. Keep in mind that there are many therapists who are not aware of the manipulative tactics of toxic family systems, or the complex dynamics of abandonment and trauma-bonding involved, who may carelessly invalidate your experience. Many therapists will erroneously address only your response to the abuse, rather than the abuse itself. It is scary for many professionals to feel as if they are going against the cultural definition of family.

Further, you have had enough experience to know your family members will largely sanitize their image in front of a therapist by putting on a façade for them. Sadly, this sanitized version of who they are is often powerful enough to sway a therapist's perception.

Therefore a second self-care step may be necessary to make sure you first choose individual therapy to do the work that needs to be done on yourself, because the focus on you in that work is guaranteed. Family therapy is rarely effective when family members are manipulative and set themselves above reproach. Your family members will be content in a therapy process as long as the problems are cast your way and they feel the therapist is in agreement with them. However, when it comes time for your family members to look at themselves and take responsibility for their behavior, they will become nasty and terminate treatment immediately.

Moment of Insight: Communication is not the key to successful relationships. Comprehension is. It does not matter how much you communicate with someone if they are committed to their own narrow and inflexible narrative.

The self-care advice you need from others, especially professionals, is to stop continually trying to fix your unfixable problems with your family members. If you expect that by your using a different set of words, better examples, and a different tone of voice, eventually your family will come around to understanding and accepting you, know that they will not. Anyone who encourages you to perfect yourself to fit in with dysfunction moves sharply against what is healthy or good for you. This type of advice is deeply destructive. It doubles the dose of your poison rather than offering its antidote. The antidote is to care enough for yourself and your overall well-being to remove whoever or whatever is harming you. This is your right.

Here are the skills that will help you master self-care:

- *Respect your limits.* Become mindful of when you are taking on too much, apologizing too much, agonizing too much, giving too much, or not asking for enough in return. It is okay to delegate some of what you need to do to those who are available and eager to help.

- *Get enough rest.* Being a good sleeper is not a reality for most people raised in an abusive family system. Anxiety and sleep unfortunately do not partner well. Listen to your body, and train yourself to rest with the use of apps or other proven sleep methods. The more rest you get, the more emotionally grounded you'll feel and the more energy you'll have available to sustain you throughout the day.

- *Eat healthy food.* Food is an opportunity to nourish yourself. As a rule of thumb, the more naturally colorful your food, the more nutrition you are supplying to your body, mind, and spirit. What you feed your stomach is what you feed your brain. If you want healthy nourishing thoughts, a feeling of vitality, and the ability to manage your emotions, you must feed your body well.

- *Exercise.* Exercise has proven time and time again to be better at stimulating the mood hormones than psychotropic medications. Further, exercise increases the neuroplasticity of the brain, which keeps you functioning at full potential. Movement, no matter how you choose to move, is also a creative outlet for your emotions, providing a physical outlet of expression and release.

- *Take life breaks.* It is important to take mini time-outs during the day. Most of those who come from psychologically abusive families are highly sensitive. This means you require periods of alone time to recharge, because you are naturally more stimulated and aware of pain, noise, lighting, smells, environmental changes, and social nuances than the average person.

- *Explore self-examination.* Take time to get to know yourself. Most survivors of toxic families are deeply thoughtful and sensing people. It is amazing how much one can experience emotionally in just one day. In these softer, self-examined moments you are reminded of how worthy the work is to love who you are.

- *Have fun.* Due to your upbringing, it is easy to take life too seriously. You were raised feeling that some type of final exam you had to pass was lurking around every corner, or else there would be hell to pay. It is important that you let your hair down and spend time playing, either happily in your own company or around people you love and enjoy. Play!

- *Nurture your spirit.* No matter what that means to you—yoga, worship, meditation, mindfulness, prayer, time in nature, reading, or journaling—make sure to take time to foster your spirit. When you do this, you realize there is a part of you that is perfect; that this part of you is above your pain and in no need of change.

Importantly, self-care includes being proud of who you have been and who you are becoming. Be so very proud of the decisions you have had to make, willingly or not, to remove yourself from the shaming abuses of your family. Be proud you took your bravery beyond the decision to sever ties, into healing. Because you deserve wonderful things like these:

- To be happy

- To be and feel secure

- To be loved by people who adore you

- To feel the safety of predictability in your relationships

- To be loved and supported in your passions

- To be held up when you are feeling down

- The freedom to be your whole True Self

- Deep and wonderful connections

- To be honored, told the truth, and treated with loving-kindness

- To be treated with respect

- To have a life of happiness and fulfillment

You deserve all of this and much, much more. Your real healing is not about making the decision to sever ties. That was only the first step. The most courageous work is happening now, after the decision has been made and you face being in this world without a family. Making this heroic self-care decision allows you to redeem your life, your self-worth, and your self-respect; and to gain the invaluable knowledge of what and who you will and will not tolerate as an influential presence in your life. Feeling deserving, knowing what you deserve, and reminding yourself of this often is the ultimate self-care. Because when you have an idea of what you deserve, you can start establishing the healthy and loving connections you have always been seeking.

Chapter 12

The Path to Your Deepest, Most Lasting Connection

Learning to be vulnerable is the path to establishing deep and lasting connections. Brené Brown discusses "excruciating vulnerability" when she describes how in order for an emotional connection to develop between yourself and someone else, you must allow yourself to be seen. Yet to be seen likely makes you feel *vul-ner-able,* especially when you are programmed to believe you have always been too much of something bad or too little of something good. Toxic shame and self-doubt have caused you to inhibit and protect your emotions rather than open them up. Yet Brown says that people who feel a true sense of their worth all have one thing in common: they live unreservedly. People who truly know their worth have the courage to be imperfect; whereas, coming from a highly dysfunctional family, you try too hard for perfection. With courage, and compassion for yourself, you will gain the ability to create deep and lasting relationships.

> **Take a Moment for You:** Reflect on what having the courage to be imperfect would mean for your life. If you allowed yourself to be vulnerable, would you try new things? Meet new types of people? Experience new ways of living, including living unreservedly? If you lived in this way, how do you imagine your life would be different?

Learning to Embrace Vulnerability

In the past, when I thought about the concept of vulnerability, it would bring a horrifying vision of being naked in front of a crowd of people and having someone circle my fat in red lipstick. Vulnerability is a word that confronts many of us with our deepest insecurities. There is no such thing as vulnerability in manipulative families. In these families, the only viable choice is to be self-protective. Abusers abuse you in your most vulnerable places, so your vulnerabilities must be pushed deeply down or otherwise masked to prevent exposing them.

Healing requires you to open these protected places. Vulnerability requires giving yourself permission to feel weak, needy, scared, or furious. Your vulnerabilities do not need to be things you feel ashamed of. Embracing them helps spare you the effort of hiding, pretending, overcompensating, or covering for the events and emotions that make you who you are. What a relief!

Moment of Insight: Embrace the opportunity to change your mindset. Your weaknesses do not make you burdensome; rather, your insecurities make you perfectly, relatably human.

Nothing in life will ever make you feel more vulnerable than manipulation, rejection, or heartbreak. Incorporate this knowledge into the person you are. When you come from a toxic family, the triggers to heartbreak are deep. When you lose a love relationship as an adult, not only do you feel the wound from the current loss, but it also reopens the cumulative heartbreaks you have experienced from people who never should have had a role in breaking your heart. For an adult survivor of a toxic family, it can be difficult to discern where old wounds stop and the current wound starts. This does not mean you are not healed. It means you will always be healing.

The Invaluable Lessons of Heartbreak

Heartbreak guarantees that your wounds of insecurity will be exposed. Heartbreak—the loss of something or someone you love—is nothing short of traumatic. So I want to share a personal story of hope.

In my most recent passage through heartbreak, I came to realize something incredibly special about myself. It awakened me to the idea that I have likely always been seeking a partner who would kiss and love my hurt places back to life. I sought this because deep down I was taught to believe that my healing needed to come from someone else's love for me. My fantasy that someone else's love would have the power to heal me fed the idea that this was what I needed to be marked as a person who was valuable, lovable, and worthy in the world. As a result, I have given other people credit for my healing and for the woman I have worked so hard to become. But it was credit they did not deserve.

I believe my old pattern of needing to give others credit for the work I have done on myself came from a deeper desire to be saved by someone in the way a healthy parent would do anything to protect and save their child. Maybe I gave this credit away to please others, to make them feel like a hero. Perhaps if they felt like a hero around me, that I needed them, they would fall so in love with that "hero feeling" that it would keep them attached to me. This makes sense, considering I learned so young that it was my responsibility to make my family members feel good about themselves, especially after their most abusive moments. Whereas my own needs were met most often with annoyance and frustration.

Swimming through the depths of my grief over this most recent relationship loss, I fortunately landed in a beautiful moment of self-discovery: I realized the only person who has ever truly kissed and loved me back to life was, is, and has always been me. However, because healing did not feel good, I had always assumed I was not healing, even though I was in the throes of doing all I could to help myself. A misconception I had about healing was that if the work I was doing did not feel good, I was not doing the work correctly. I made the false assumption that I was not progressing; that my healing would feel good, real, or valid only if it came from the person or people who broke me. It is strange that we seek to be healed by the exact sources of our pain. Heartbreak is tricky.

Unfortunately, this unconscious habit of giving others credit for my emotional work served only to get me walked on by many who claimed to love me, and I cannot really blame them. They did not deserve the power of healing me, but I gave it to them, and I gave this power generously. It makes me feel sad now, in hindsight, because these people did nothing to earn a position in my life elevated above my own personal authority and significance. *By my doing this, I created the space for them to treat me recklessly, to take advantage of me, and they did. Why wouldn't they? What a lesson.*

I will forever treasure this precious moment of realizing the most trusted and loving relationship I have always had, that has always been there for me without fail and with consistency, is my relationship with myself. This understanding has been earth-shattering. I am the person who has sat with myself in my hardest, most private, and most devastating moments, and it was me who had to comfort and coach myself through thoughts of self-hate and feelings of abandonment, self-doubt, heartbreak, and shame.

On the heels of this heartbreak, I made an agreement with myself to no longer give anyone credit for my healing or for where I am at in my life. Today I will thank and lovingly acknowledge the amazing people who have been generous with their time and unconditional love and support, but I cannot credit them for my growth, nor would they want or need that from me.

Like me, you may never have known you could give yourself credit, that you are worthy of it. I certainly received more put-downs than credit from my family, and I wholeheartedly believed their version of me because I was a child. All children believe their parents. What other choice do we have? As I have matured, somewhere deep within I did not know I deserved credit for healing the mess I was raised to believe I was. It is liberating to be able to own the power I have used to change my life. You can own this power too.

> **Moment of Insight:** No one can love or heal you better than you can, because the only thing you are an expert on, the person you must know the deepest and love the most, is and should always be you.

Take a Moment for You: Reflect on how you experience heartbreak. Have you given other people the power to make you feel whole? How has that worked? What lessons have you learned?

The Truth About Emotional Strength

Many people say to me, "You're so strong," with regard to boundaries I have set on my destructive family and other relationships to be a healthy person. There is a part of me that absolutely identifies that I am strong, and I appreciate that others admire this trait in me. However, there is a truth beneath "being strong" that many do not realize. I will acknowledge that, most often, I do the brave *thing*. I recognize I do the things that most avoid, but in all humility, I do *not* do those brave things bravely. I do them because I feel that I *have* to, not because I *want* to. What may look strong from the outside may not always be how I feel on the inside, especially when I am having to make the brave decision. Most often, I do these brave things feeling shattered, uncertain, terrified, confused, and broken.

Take a Moment for You: Reflect on how you feel when you are making the brave but excruciating decisions to save your mental health and well-being. How do you feel when people tell you that you are strong?

Being brave is even more challenging when you have very little connection to your family. There are few things more paralyzing than making bold decisions to leave your toxic nonfamilial relationships as an adult, because you then must face the uncertainty of being completely alone. You may even trick yourself into believing that you are the common denominator in all your problematic relationships. Truthfully, you are a *part* of that problem, in that your trauma has resulted in your being a "bad picker." However, if you're getting yourself out of emotionally abusive relationships, you are still doing the right and brave thing, even if it's not making you feel good in the short term.

I get that it is hard to feel as if you're ever really healing when even being brave doesn't feel good. You have been brave to leave any relationship, but you're still left with the pain of that loss, which can make you feel your wounds never get a real chance to recover. One heartbreak seemingly just builds on another and another.

This is the process of healing from deep childhood trauma. This is what your healing will look like, so it is important to accept that heartbreak will be an integral part of your journey. It is through your most challenging times that you grow. You cannot grow when everything is good. You cannot become the radiant and powerful person you are meant to be without heartbreak being a significant part of that journey.

Are Deep Wounds Totally Recoverable?

When any type of heartbreak rocks my world, I do question if it is completely possible to heal the tragic lack of self-worth that survivors embrace, at the very heart of our being. Knowing how the brain is developed with the amygdala and hippocampal structures, I do not believe that deep wounds around emotional abuse are *totally* recoverable. Instead, I believe that they have the potential to grow you into a stronger and more valiant warrior each time they are triggered. I believe that you can achieve a sense of worth or value over time and through experiences such as your achievements, failures, and heartbreaks; and through being able to get back up again, improve your skill set and mindset, grow your family, choose healthier relationships, and nurture a deeper sense of love and respect for who you are as a person.

Yet it seems there is this nagging space deep down that makes us question whether we are truly worthy or good enough. We are hardwired to believe that love is something we must earn and work hard to keep. At the precipice of any real loss or rejection, this lack of self-worth seems to rise from our depths no matter how much we do or have done to heal it.

So what do you do with this? You stand for the sense of self-worth you cannot feel in these shattered moments. I find that I seem to stand the strongest for myself when I am at my bottom line. There I recognize that I am the only one there for me, so I am all I've got. I am the only one I have to turn to. This is how it always has been and always will be. I can trust this. I choose to keep going and to focus on the next step in front of me.

Take a Moment for You: Reflect on whether you are there for yourself at the bottom line. If so, how are you there for yourself?

Perhaps this sense of low self-worth is something you can start to view as central to who you are. Instead of labeling this part of you as "bad," choose to see it as a vulnerable but deeply lovable aspect of your whole person—the aspect of you that is your teacher, that keeps you going and growing, that you will always need to coach, honor, protect, and nurture.

So as you traverse this world, filled with people you will—and will not—want to be part of your life, first honor your primary relationship: the one with yourself. You will be there for yourself regardless of what happens with others, and the more you can support yourself unconditionally, the more you will share your True Self with others. The day you can be your vulnerable True Self with others is the day you will most appreciate how far you have helped yourself come.

You have learned that you can depend on yourself in the ways you needed and wanted to depend upon your family. This level of self-care will help you navigate the abuses that are sure to come in the aftermath of cutting ties.

PART 3

practical
ways to
handle
the
aftermath

Chapter 13

Family Members Can Continue to Be Vindictive

This chapter offers a warning: Even though you have cut ties and put different levels of firm boundaries in place, and your personal healing is well under way, all this will effect little change in your toxic family and their mode of operation. So it is imperative you understand the reasons your family members are the way they are. Perhaps not being sick enough to understand them can be seen as a gift. However, the more you learn, the more the information sinks in; the deeper your understanding grows, the greater your potential to become healthy and whole.

> **Moment of Insight:** The greatest trick the devil ever played was to convince people he didn't exist.

When it comes to psychologically abusive family systems, knowledge is power. Personal education is a giant, continual, and critical part of your growth. You need to be reminded, again and again, that the problem, or the source of your family members' spiteful treatment, was never a result of you personally, but rather a result of their own deeply flawed characters. At their core, psychologically dysfunctional people suffer from self-hatred and a deep internalized shame. As you build your knowledge about your family members, understand that their own trauma never entitled them to reenact it on you.

If you try to approach your understanding of toxic people as you would approach understanding healthy people, you will only become more confused. It's easier if you view toxic people's makeup as the polar opposite of yours. Being a person of empathy, you care about others first, whereas toxic people care about themselves first. In relationships, you care about how you make the other person feel, and they care about how they make you feel. You're focused on what you can give; toxic people care about how much they can get.

Counterintuitive

When it comes to your family, it takes only one word to understand what you are dealing with: "counterintuitive." How your family presents themselves on the surface has little to do with who they are underneath. Recall our discussion of family billboards. The billboard of the toxic family can be broken down to a lie; a false advertisement offering something that may look great on the surface but on the inside is horribly dysfunctional. I cannot tell you how many patients of mine have said to me, "No one would ever believe how twisted my family is; everyone loves them." In reality, your family members are more like hunters. They hunt for power in the form of attention and emotional reaction.

Predation and Scorekeeping

Family systems that function around coercion have a rapacious, scorekeeping approach to their social world and family life. Their children are not exempt from their manipulative ways. In fact, it is the children who experience the worst of their abuse—because it's easy to gain power over someone smaller, more defenseless, and completely dependent upon you. Children have neither the psychological development nor the ability to process concepts like "manipulation" or "emotional abuse." As a child, you could not comprehend that your family members spend nearly all their mental energy in an unspoken competition with everyone they meet. This includes you. They view themselves as having to fight off potential threats to their fragile egos and endlessly prove themselves to be better and more powerful than those around them. This scorekeeping approach means they have little peace as they make their way through life, which incites them to wreak holy hell in the lives of others, especially yours. The only needs that matter to your family members are their own.

Winners Versus Losers

For your family there are only two ways to present themselves: as winners or losers. Because they view the world from a place of scarcity, they do whatever it takes to make sure they are one of the winners. They cannot tolerate being put down or overlooked. For example, in a group of people they will feel put down if someone other than them receives a compliment. This fills them with jealousy and hatred of the person complimented. They become preoccupied with getting rid of the praised person, even if that person is their child.

Sadly, any threat to their fragile ego must be identified and erased immediately. If the threat continues, it must be annihilated by any means necessary. Your family members feel the most threatened when someone says or does something that makes them feel small, weak, or flawed. If anyone puts them down or humiliates them, they will unleash rage at a level they've been stoking for decades and will not let up until they have verbally or emotionally ruined their target. This retaliatory impulse underlies the abuses your family sets in motion after you cut ties. People who have not been in a close relationship with a severely toxic person would never believe the ugly, animalistic wrath that spews from them when they are activated. If they believe you have crossed them, you will become their most sought-after perceived offender. To make you pay for what you have done to them, there is no level they will not stoop to.

When you are the focus of their abusive ways, it is scary, not because you cannot stand up for yourself, but because of how malicious and volatile they can be. You must accept there are no limits your family will not cross. Seeking to destroy their perceived adversaries is simply par for the course. Even so, when these people are family, it is nearly impossible to get used to this type of emotional violence. After you cut ties, you hope that they will eventually tire of your silence and go pick on someone else. Unfortunately, the wound to their ego—when someone of their own blood has the audacity to stand up to them—enrages them.

When you are the one who leaves, you can be sure your family will not allow you to walk away easily, so you must prepare for how you will handle your family dynamics post cutting ties. The next chapter will help you anticipate and prepare for the common challenges.

Chapter 14

Handling Secondary Abuse:
Gifts and Cards, Financial Abuse,
and Family Illness and Death

Based on my own aftermath, and witnessing that of my patients, you will quickly learn that just because contact stops on your end, usually the abuse and manipulation doesn't stop on your family's end, although it may drastically slow down or change in form. I'm going to help you understand many of the ways your family will work to gain access to your life regardless of limits you have set in place. I will highlight some of their favorite and most-used tactics and provide examples and solutions to help you navigate these issues.

Secondary Abuse

Secondary abuse is the reaction secondary people have to their not being able to see, understand, or verify the abuses of your family when they are directly happening to you. Secondary people are outside observers of the relationship who often cannot recognize the insidiousness of emotional abuse, even when it is directly in front of them. Secondary abuse occurs when these secondary people inadvertently blame, criticize, and question your reactions to the hidden abuses they may not be able to see. Many of them will try to "talk sense into you." Their questioning and pressuring is secondary abuse. Secondary abuse also occurs when people who do not know you personally join in the family warfare against you because they have been tainted to believe you are a horrible person. Because of their tainted mindset toward you, they will carelessly contribute to your abuse.

Your toxic family members will almost always join forces in bullying to intimidate you. This chapter shares three common areas of secondary abuse: gifts and cards, financial abuse, and illness and death.

Gifts and Cards

After you have established no contact, your family may try to sneak back into your life by sending presents or cards. The words and gifts sent typically have a cryptic and passive-aggressive undertone not always recognizable to others. In my first two years of estrangement, the cards sent my way were filled with sickly-sweet messages, drastically incongruent with the current state of the relationship. The gifts and cards glossed over my trauma as if it had never happened. You need to recognize that overly dramatized verbal expressions or extravagant gifts that blatantly ignore the real abuses at hand do not suffice for genuine apologies or count toward repairing the relationship. Your family members are experts at using fake sentiment to try to accomplish this.

Moment of Insight: Your predatory family members transmit abuse in packages that look like love.

The real reason your estranged family members pursue you with gifts and cards is to uphold their "good person" image and to build the credibility of the story they tell of your cruelty toward them. They send these items for their own manipulative purposes, not for any benefit to you. Secondary observers such as your friends, children, cousins, aunts, uncles, or romantic partners may not see through the sickly-sweet sentiment and will buy into it, saying that your family is at least trying. It's hard for these people to understand that your family members prefer to *look* good rather than to *be* good. When unsuspecting people buy into the fake sentiment, they erroneously conclude you are the bad guy; some may even confront you for being nonresponsive to your family's efforts. The erroneous assumptions and conclusions of those external to your situation are secondary abuse.

In the aftermath, you should aim to reach a point where other people's believing your family's false story of you and/or seeing their false sentiment as a genuine effort is simply part of the journey, because you understand there is nothing for you to defend. It is not an effective use of your time or mental and emotional energy trying to win over anyone who is committed to believing lies about you. You know the truth of your family. If love and respect are not going to be served, you have the right to leave the table. You do not owe anyone an explanation.

Financial Abuse

Financial abuse is a favorite form of secondary abuse that your family will likely use in some form. It is common in psychologically abusive family systems to weaponize money throughout their child-rearing. You are rarely given anything without their later using it as leverage to induce feelings of guilt and obligation. Children in toxic family systems are treated more like a commodity to be possessed than as persons with needs, wants, desires, and feelings of their own. In this type of dynamic, money is traded for compliance. This approach to being a family lacks logic and is riddled with manipulation. Many toxic parents view paying for the things their children need as a sacrifice rather than a normal part of parenting.

In my office I have heard of parents complaining about having to pay for necessities like shampoo or food. As a child of such parents, you are consistently left feeling the money spent on you is a burden, not because the family is short on funds and needs to conserve, but because you are not worthy of it. Sadly, long into adulthood you have a difficult time accepting anything, including help, from anyone. Unfortunately, when you receive, you reflexively feel like you owe. Thus you deny the people who love you the positive feelings they hope for when they contribute to your life.

Most people I know or have treated have been financially supported, helped, or gifted by family in some way on and off throughout their life. None of these individuals have been overly indulged or enabled. Financial abuse is not about spoiled or entitled adults cutting ties with family to manipulate their family members to give in to their unreasonable financial demands. Why do healthy family members—parents, grandparents, or even siblings and other extended family members—choose to financially contribute to those they love long into adulthood? Because healthy family members want to make sure the people they love, no matter their age, have what they need. Healthy family members who have the means enjoy contributing to the success and happiness of those they love by offering support during critical times, milestones, or transitions. Unfortunately, once you sever ties, money becomes an effective way for your family members to manipulate you.

Allow me to share a personal example of financial abuse, with the sole intention of demonstrating how the smear campaign set against you, post cutting ties, influences the objectivity of those hired to manage trusts and wills, and what options are available when/if you face this in your own life.

Recently, I was manipulated with a family trust left by my grandmother. To my surprise, the woman who manages my grandmother's trust sent paperwork stating that my sibling and I would be receiving quarterly statements and could start drawing from the principal. The trust was written to give a family member of mine full discretionary power to decide how my grandmother's money was spent, even though my grandmother was clear she wanted her money used to support the educational needs of the generations to come—namely the children my sibling and I would bring into the world.

I made the trust manager aware that this family member and I did not have a healthy connection and expressed my concern this would influence unanimous agreements made by my request, the bank, and this family member. The manager assured me she was trained to be objective and fair; however, what I saw in the numbers with regard to withdrawals taken from the principal was deeply revealing with regards to this person and her own spending, and it also revealed that my sibling had already taken two substantial disbursements for his child's expensive private high school tuition. One of my sibling's withdrawals was taken a year before I was told disbursements could be taken out.

To test the waters, I requested disbursements for my daughter's education equal to what my sibling had taken for his child, to be placed in an account to be managed by the same bank as the trust so they could verify I would not spend any of the money on myself. The emails I sent with this request were not even given the courtesy of a professional response to let me know the bank and my family member were not unanimous. My emails were ignored. Being ignored by the manager of the trust was textbook secondary abuse. My family had recruited them to join in their manipulative agenda against me.

I was advised by those who care about me to seek legal advice, which initially I did not want to do. However, I went to see an attorney purely to prove to my supports that what I knew to be true was in fact true. My grandmother's money was being used for manipulation.

The family member in power views taking these actions against me as totally just. She would rather seek revenge by threatening my daughter's educational future than offer a sincere apology or show some level of humanity or fairness to work things out between us. The trust paperwork was sent to me because that person wants me to see the power she holds to take from my child resources that were intended to be hers. Where this person is wrong is that she cannot take anything she wants away from me or my child, because she cannot take our dignity.

When your perception of the abuse you're experiencing is questioned by those you love, this unfortunately is also secondary abuse. You realize that people think you are irrational and naïve, rather than wisely perceptive about the type of manipulation that's happening.

Here are three tips for addressing financial abuse:

1. See the game being played (this is critical).

2. Seek legal advice to define your course of action or inaction.

3. Move forward with composure and close the circle to protect yourself.

Here is how I brought closure to my family's attempt to manipulate me financially. I hope it serves as an example or template to copy if you are feeling stuck, not knowing what to do in this type of situation. I sent the following email to the manager of the trust.

Dear....

After leaving my attorney today, I am aware that although I have rights to this trust and the money my grandmother intended for myself and my daughter, I also have no power to benefit from it because [the family member with discretionary power] is your client, not me. I now understand why you are not responding to any of my emails requesting to receive equal disbursements of money for my daughter's educational future as my sibling is taking out for his children. For this reason, I have no desire to receive quarterly statements to see what I am being pushed out of, which is this individual's intention.

I will happily, humbly, and abundantly take care of myself and my daughter. For us, love is the most powerful form of currency we share and value.

If, at the time of this person's death, my sibling has not gone through all the money and there is any money left in my grandmother's trust, I will put that money in an account for my daughter.

I wish you the best,

Dr. Sherrie Campbell

I hope this story has been helpful and educational. This is just one of many ways to handle the financial abuse you are likely to face at some point post cutting ties. Keep in mind that financial abuse is one of a toxic person's favorite ways to manipulate.

Shannon Thomas, author of *Exposing Financial Abuse: When Money Is a Weapon*, tells us that when money is being used as a weapon, this type of abuse is unlimited when toxic people are either passively or overtly controlling all the resources. It also happens when toxic people limit access to bank accounts and trusts and/or refuse to contribute equally.[21] When it comes to financial abuse, the idea of cutting off a child (no matter their age) financially is intensely frightening. This person in my life talked about this trust for my future so often that, even though I have a successful career, it was comforting to feel a sense of security outside of my own income for my daughter, just in case anything happened to me.

Fortunately, when faced with something like financial abuse or the manipulation of monies from a trust, you do have options. I have treated patients who have chosen to take legal action; others went back into the toxic family dynamic, at least temporarily and cordially, to protect themselves from losing out on monies they stood to benefit from; still others, like myself, chose to walk away from the money altogether. You must analyze your own unique situation and choose the option that fits best for your bigger picture. To do this, consider the following questions and come up with your own answers.

What would a healthy family do with a will or trust? Asking this question can shed some light on how different the outcome would look with unconditional love and acceptance. A healthy parent or family member would have put an equal sum of money into an account for my daughter, matching the amount my sibling took for his child. Beyond my own example, a healthy family member would make sure to let you know that any time you felt ready to heal and talk, they would always be available; that they are deeply sorry the relationship is in such a bad place and for their part in that.

> **Moment of Insight:** With a healthy parent or family member there would be no games, no coercion, and no acting out.

When you walk away from money, does your family "win"? Your family uses money for secondary abuse because the god they worship, the thing that gives them power, is printed green paper. Money is their god because it allows them to *play* god; to maintain manipulative control over their children, siblings, grandchildren, and other family members. The primary goal of financial abuse is to stop you from taking the key steps you need to in order to move away from them. Fortunately, money is not your god, and you never need to sell your soul to have money. Undoubtedly, if you choose to walk away from money, there are people who will think you have let your family win. Some will believe that for you to win, you need to go after what your family is blocking you from rightfully receiving. Keep in mind, severing ties is not about winning or losing. You either have freedom and happiness, or you don't. You need to simply not care whether other people think you've let your family win. In fact, I do not care if my family thinks they won. I did not lose anything. I have everything they do not: my freedom and my happiness.

Illness and Death

Another form of secondary abuse crops up with the mental and/or medical issues your toxic family members face as they age. You cannot predict with any accuracy how you will feel in these pivotal moments. Nearly every survivor of a toxic family will confront news about the failing health or impending death of their family members. Your toxic family members will use this as a golden opportunity to reinsert themselves into your life. Here's how they do it.

USE OF THIRD-PARTY "INFORMERS"

To start, your family will likely choose someone close to you to give you the news. If that does not work, they will choose a different, more peripheral person to catch you off guard. Your family will approach this person with the story that there was no other way to contact you other than through them, because you have "cut them off." This false story sets up your secondary abuse before you are even contacted. Your family wants to put you in the uncomfortable position of having to explain yourself to a person with whom you would otherwise not share any of these intimate details—that is, your choices around no contact, and what you will or will not do in this deathbed situation. Your family wants your decisions to be open to their scrutiny, to humiliate you and make it appear as if you lack basic human decency. Their choice of a person to give you the news and their unwanted opinion is irrelevant. This is secondary abuse.

In this type of situation, mail is an appropriate way to get information to you. As you know, your emotionally needy family members live for the dramatic. It makes sense, then, that your family would not use the option of mail or request a medical professional or attorney to reach out to you, because that would not feed their need for direct power or control. Unfortunately for my family, when the person they chose to give me the news about my father's impending death asked them for more detail on the status of his illness—in order to best support and inform me, considering the gravity of what he was about to tell me—my family snidely informed him that if I wanted any details on my father's health, I would need to contact them. My father's looming death was being used as a tool to break my no-contact boundaries. There really is no low too low for toxic family members to use to get what they want, while setting the stage to make you look like the bad guy.

FINDING OUT IN SOCIAL MEDIA OR ONLINE

I learned of my dad's death through Google, two weeks after his passing and two days before his service. My family believes the decision to not tell me of his passing is justifiable and what I had coming to me. This type of inhumane treatment is nearly impossible to explain to others who have no experience with this type of toxicity.

Many erroneously believe that after we've established no contact, when a toxic family member dies it shouldn't impact us. We are essentially blamed for our own pain because *we* put up boundaries to that relationship.

Remember: we each have the right to set boundaries to protect our own mental health and well-being.

I think the deaths of toxic family members are a singular kind of hard. Those who grew up in a healthy family are left knowing they were always loved; they have a lifetime of positive memories to revisit and take comfort in. They are memories worth keeping alive. However, when a toxic family member dies, you are left with the pain, horrible memories, and having to hold this turmoil and make sense of it, even as you are in the process of healing.

Your saving grace is understanding that healing is always an inside job. If we make our healing dependent on another's validation of their mistreatment of us, healing will not be possible. In that case, we are left with our suffering as we wait for something that will never come.

Healing happens when we decide to heal. Healing happens when we decide to find the meaning in our suffering. Healing is active and forward-moving. Grief, too, is an active process. Creating happiness is always an active process.

Feel what you need to feel.

Deal with your circumstances as they unfold.

Heal your heart with self-care and self-compassion.

Forward is a pace.

NOT CONTACTING TOXIC FAMILY MEMBERS WHEN THERE IS A DEATH

If you learn that one of those you severed contact with has died, take a moment to just breathe. You are not obligated to contact your abusive family members on the occasion of a death in the family. The person who told me my father was dying did provide my father's contact information—with the side note that my father had mentioned in the recent past that he did not want to be contacted! After much thought and consideration, I made the choice to not contact my father, especially knowing this was his wish. Further, my father's last words to me seven years prior had been horribly abusive and threatening. He had hung up on me, and I'd not heard from him since. On that day, I knew in my gut that we had had our last interaction, because this is how life was with him. He would rage and cut me off for years until I was pressured by my other family members to fix things with him. Throughout my life with my father, he made it my responsibility to fix our relationship, to forgive him and make him feel good, which time and again set me up for further abuse. So why or how could I ever feel safe contacting him?

> **Take a Moment for You:** Reflect on the thoughts and feelings that come up when you envision facing this situation. Do you feel guilty? Do you feel afraid? If so, why?

IT IS NOT YOUR JOB TO CLEAR ANYONE'S CONSCIENCE

From a space of objectivity, my father's journey through cancer—which apparently was long and slow—never inspired him to reach out and repair the relationship with me. Therefore I could not see what was so critically different now that he was on his deathbed. He'd had years and years to work things out with me. Further, I had no idea what response I would get if I did contact him, and I was not willing to put myself back in that scary, volatile, and unpredictable place. Experience tells me he would have more than likely sought to hurt me. If, by chance, he'd shown a loving side, I cannot see how it could be genuine. He would be using my vulnerability and natural pull toward him as my father to escape accountability on the one-yard line before he passed away.

I certainly did not wish for him to die in emotional pain, yet whether his conscience was clear or not was a burden I could not allow him or anyone else to place under my control. Dying with a clear conscience was personal work he needed to accomplish during and throughout his life, and he'd had ample opportunity to do so. Just because he was dying did not change who he was.

My father did not get a lobotomy; he got cancer. He had destroyed nearly every relationship and career opportunity placed in his life. I chose not to put myself or my heart in a position that I would never place my own child in: to be used or emotionally abused by him again simply because he was dying. All that should matter to my father was that I am genuinely happy in my life.

You will face your own particular situation when it comes to the death of your toxic family members. There is no right and wrong in this situation, no formula that can be universally applied to everyone. Search your heart and do what is best for you, whatever that may be. Further, you do not owe anyone an explanation for the choices you make.

Moment of Insight: Death does not change people. Choosing to change is what changes people.

ARE YOU "HEARTLESS" TO KEEP NO-CONTACT BOUNDARIES UP AROUND DEATH?

If you choose to keep your boundaries and remain distant at the time of a death, this does not mean you are heartless. In fact, it was extremely painful to hear that my father was dying. Far from heartless, it was heart-wrenching. I do not believe any child is prepared to hear their parent or any family member is going to die, no matter the relationship they had or did not have. It is devastating. When I found out my father was dying, I had to process a myriad of unexpected emotions. Memories of the father he was started coursing through my mind, forcing me to revisit all the pain and damage he had caused in tandem with feeling the happiness I felt in some of the rare, happier, more hopeful moments we had shared. I also found myself haunted with visions of him on his deathbed. It was upsetting.

I have been afraid of my father since my earliest memory, due to his explosive nature and frequent outbursts of rage. I found myself picturing him frail and ill, and it made me feel sorry for him, but it also filled me with anxiety. I had strange feelings that made no logical sense—like that when he passed away I would no longer have any privacy. It felt like death would give him unlimited access to my life, which felt eerie and out of my control. I also found myself feeling terrified of being misunderstood by others because I chose not to contact him. The thought of calling him made me feel sick with fear. Everything in my body resisted, not out of stubbornness, but from a history of knowing he is not a safe person.

Nevertheless, he was my dad, and now there was no more hope for us, but…there never was. I lived my entire life with a huge hole in my heart where his loving, supportive, strong presence should have been. That did not change for me because he was dying. It just made the hole permanent. But it also brought me peace, because he could no longer hurt me, and perhaps that opened a door for some sort of connection I could have with him in death that I wasn't able to have in life. My only hope for my father is that he rest in peace.

As you go through these varying manipulations intended to compromise your freedom, accept that they hurt. It's okay that it hurts. These abuses are designed to be hurtful. Let's examine why.

Why Does Secondary Abuse Hurt?

Secondary abuse hurts because no one has the power to wound us more deeply than family. Family is not supposed to be this way. There is no getting used to hurts like fake sentiments and gifts, financial abuse, or manipulations around illness and death with any sense of comfort—let alone being intentionally placed in a position of feeling you must explain to others why and how these covert actions done to you are abusive. This is exhausting. What you develop as you heal is wisdom. The surest sign you have moved into a healthier psychological space is when you have no desire to respond to your family's exploitations of you, no matter how hurtful and provoking they may be. Further, you lose all desire to explain yourself to people who judge you.

> **Moment of Insight:** When you can walk away from your family's ploys to suck you back in, you have succeeded.

Practicing acceptance is perhaps the most effective tool when facing the harsher realities of life. You must come to accept negative realities, thoughts, and emotions as a natural part of life, to view them as necessary for healthy psychological functioning. To do this you must take an active part in defining your own goals and values, then live those goals and values with commitment.

Here are ways to heal from secondary abuse:

- *View secondary abuse as a reminder.* The negative reality of secondary abuse includes an important gift: the reminder that your toxic family members will continue to be invasive and deceptive regardless of the estrangement. The powerful equalizers of acceptance and humility allow you to use the abuses inflicted on you as springboards to becoming a better person, with values that do not include manipulating, hurting, or seeking pointless revenge on others, including your family.

- *Know what to expect, so you can accept.* Hope in a toxic family dynamic can be deadly. To stay healthy, you must accept that your family members are not likely to change, irrespective of the hard evidence that it would be in their best interest to do so. When you expect abuse, you are better prepared to handle it.

- *Practice composure.* The most effective response to manipulation is to not engage. Never reward a destructive person's negative actions with your negative reaction. Trust that fighting back is at best inflicting additional wounds. To avoid this, practice composure instead.

- *Remember that silence is key.* You must accept that your family will go to any length to lurk in the corners of your life—where you do not even realize you lack protection—in order to sneak their abuses across your boundaries. They do this to produce shock and to wreak havoc on the peace and balance you are striving to create. When the shock comes, your superpower is to remain silent. There is no long-term benefit in doing anything else.

- *Process, rather than deny, emotional pain.* When you process your emotions and move them toward acceptance, you gain the knowledge and understanding to no longer participate in the drama. The personal and spiritual self-examination you must undergo is tremendous, but well worth it. Whatever you can process, you can overcome.

Now it's time to apply all that you have been learning to your current life. Healing is an active process that you must commit to every day for the long-term stability of your life. When you make healing an active and alive process, you can expect these results:

- You become wise by learning from experience.

- You invest more deeply in your self-development.

- You do not skip over the hurts; instead, you feel them and accept them.

- You allow yourself to feel wounded, shocked, and disgusted at the atrocities inflicted on you by your family, so you can work toward healing them.

Toxic family members will punish you for every act of self-love you take away from them, because they want control. In the spirit of loving yourself, untether yourself from the family members who place undue restrictions on your life and liveliness. No one, and I mean no one, has the right to impinge upon your right to be the person you need, want, and desire to be. *No one* includes your family, extended family, family friends, teachers, exes, and anyone else. Be prepared for your family to insert anyone they can into their game of trying to rob you of your rights to be free from them. You'll find clear direction on preparing for this in the next chapter.

Chapter 15

The Dirty Work of Using People, Holidays, Social Media, and Major Events

When your toxic family members purposely use shared connections to create problems, they are practicing *post-separation abuse*. Your toxic family members may also use other outlets, such as large gatherings or social media, as avenues to cross your boundaries. Post-separation abuse (not to be confused with secondary abuse, which may be unintentional on the part of the people external to your situation) is a cruel form of intentional manipulation used by your family to stop you from being able to fully leave the relationship with them. Some have labeled seeking this type of control over another's life as psychological and/or emotional terrorism. With post-separation abuse, your family is sending you the message that you are not allowed to say no to them under any circumstances—and if you do, you will pay a price.

> **Take a Moment for You:** Reflect on how your family members have used others, major events, or social media to violate your boundaries.

The ways your family members may enact post-separation abuse are detailed in this chapter.

Triangulation: Using Others to Do Their Dirty Work

Although your family may not directly break through your no-contact boundaries, to further their retaliation campaign they may deliberately triangulate other people to enact their revenge. The most common term for these triangulated people in the literature is *flying monkeys*. In the book and the movie *The Wizard of Oz*, the Wicked Witch of the West had an army of flying monkeys, trusted retainers she would send out to taunt Dorothy and her crew to stop them from realizing their independent destinations, dreams, and life goals (or to outright kidnap them). The triangulated people used by your family are like these flying monkeys. They are also known in the literature as servants, minions, and lieutenants. However, I prefer to call them "messengers" because these middle people are sent your way with the sole purpose of forcing the topic of your family back into your life, regardless of boundaries you've set.

Many of these messengers, although directly involved in the abuse, have no personal malevolent intentions toward you. Your family members can be incredibly convincing and charismatic, and they heavily promote the defamatory lie that you have ruthlessly victimized them. Because your family comes across as sincere, it is nearly impossible for messengers to discern the abuser from the real victim. Messengers falsely believe that no one would ever want to harm or feel so negatively toward you unless you are truly a terrible person.

> **Moment of Insight:** Your toxic family members will train their messengers in the art of gossip and lies because they can't accomplish their hate-filled agenda of turning people against you without fabricated stories of your "lack of mental health" and made-up examples of "abuses" you have inflicted on them.

Why are the chosen messengers so naïve as to wholeheartedly believe the lies your family tells them to deliver to you? Author H. G. Tudor explains this best. In his book *Manipulated*, Tudor explains, "Toxic people are manipulating all the time; every moment of every day they are manipulating those around them. They have honed these skills over years of practice. Each day they extend their tendrils and slide them around people and bring them around to their way of thinking. This has them in a position of having people doing what they want, when they want, and doing so repeatedly."[22] The critical and truthful information your abusive family withholds from the people they triangulate is the abuse they have exacted upon you, how long you tolerated it, and how often you excused their abuse long before you chose to set healthy boundaries.

Your family members know they must choose people who sincerely believe there is "good in everyone" and who hold strong values of togetherness as it relates to the concept of family. These well-intended messengers can be any person who

- Tries to deliberately guilt or coerce you into reconnecting with your family

- Refuses to accept the idea that you need the boundaries you have set in place

- Minimizes your experience of abuse, or disputes it

- Views your boundaries as your having a problem with forgiveness or stubbornness

- Intentionally brings up your family members in conversation, knowing you are estranged from them

These well-intentioned people reason that any decent person would never unfairly abuse anyone in the ways that you claim your family has abused you; therefore, they believe they can set you straight. Your family taps into the well-intentioned person's need to be a hero, making them believe they are doing the right thing. Your family rewards their messengers for their "help" with praise, flattery, and attention.

A workable solution to this type of manipulation is to tell the messenger, "If you continue to bring my family up in our conversations or refuse to accept, acknowledge, or hear the validity of my experience in a fair and equitable manner, I will be left with no other choice but to cut ties with you as well."

There *are* family members who try to destroy the lives of their children, siblings, and others for no real reason. These types of families do exist. Too many people do not understand this, so too often the real victims are not believed; rather, they are further abused by enlisted messengers.

The Gossips

Not all shared connections used as messengers are naïve or well-intended. Sometimes your family will choose other toxic people who love gossip and drama, who enjoy being in the middle of the chaos, who have the same bad intentions toward you, and who are more than happy to get involved. Maybe they just do not like you, or maybe their goal is to fit in with your family. Either way, you must not try to confront or convince any messenger of your side of the story. No matter how much you try to explain and prove the truth or point out the errors in the flawed information these mutually shared people are operating from, they have already been poisoned and assigned their role between you and your destructive family. Your job is to step back and allow things to take their course.

You may experience a former enlisted messenger who later reaches out, apologizes, and validates that you were correct, and that they never should have allowed themselves to be so hurtfully involved. They often feel guilty for the pain they caused you with their inappropriate involvement. When or if these triangulated people surface with an apology, it is up to you whether to forgive them or not. Sometimes reconciliation is possible; other times it is not; it all depends on the severity of emotional damage they helped create in your life.

Our Loved Ones

Other sought-after messengers are the people closest to you—your spouse, ex-spouse, children, or even your closest friends. This is where the depths of betrayal can be most devastating. When your predatory family members feel entitled enough to try to use those closest to you to assert their agenda, there is nothing that will hurt you more profoundly. Your family members know this is the most violating boundary breach, but it also, by intention, puts the people you love in a toxic triangulated position.

Your family members use this tactic to make you feel betrayed by these loved ones. They seek to disrupt and fracture the supportive network you have developed; to leave you with no one, so you have no other option but to return to your family.

> **Moment of Insight:** Your primary supporters must back your decision to sever ties with your family by following suit themselves.

Your supports need to be very clear that allowing this type of triangulation—no matter how nice, innocent, or genuine it may seem, coming from your family—is violating and wrong. There is no way to have definitive boundaries with your family if they gain access to passing messages to you through your main support system.

Holidays and Major Events

Holidays and other major events serve as a point in time rather than a person or relationship to triangulate for post-separation abuse. Most survivors of toxic families who have gone no-contact have been able to effectively block family members' entrance into their life through emails, smartphones, and social media. However, if family members know your physical address, they will use mail as a third-party line of access to violate your boundaries. Psychologically abusive family members love to use holidays, birthdays, anniversaries, or family gatherings, and so on to creep in and put on their simulation of being good.

What do you do with gifts sent to your house? Many people have asked me this. Most often, the answer is *nothing*. Many survivors ask if they should send the gifts back. I would say no, unless your family uses this avenue of abuse relentlessly. In that case you can send a note telling them their gifts and cards are not welcomed and if they continue to send them, they will be returned or donated. Understand that they will likely use your returning gifts as evidence of your cruelty and abuse of them.

You also do not need to send a thank-you card if you keep a gift. Whether you send thank-you cards or not, it does not make you the better person (unless you are competing to prove yourself to be just that), nor does sending thank-you cards have any influence on quelling your family's abuses and exploitations. Your family members will abuse and manipulate, regardless of the peacekeeping actions you take, so there really is no such thing as keeping the peace. Please do not mistake my recommendation for silence as encouraging you to lose your voice or sacrifice your personal power. I encourage you to view silence as your superpower.

> **Moment of Insight:** Your toxic family members can do absolutely nothing if you do nothing.

Shared Family Events

Severing ties often means you do not attend events your family will be attending. If, however, this is unavoidable, have a plan. It can look something like this:

- Show up to the event a little late.

- Keep yourself busy with helping activities (setting up, cooking, cleaning up) so your attention is occupied.

- Plan on leaving a little early.

- At any sign of impending conflict or drama, get your things and quietly leave.

- Stay out of gossip.

- Do not engage in conversation with your abusive family members or their messengers who try to use these types of gatherings as a time to confront you.

- Have safe people there to help protect you.

But really, your best course of action is to not attend the event. Courteously inform the people who invited you that you would love to celebrate with them separately, as things are not peaceful between yourself and your family, and it is in the best interests of all involved for you to keep your distance.

Social Media

Social media is the newest and most available option for your family to use for post-separation abuse. I treated a patient, Julie, who dealt with social media abuse. Julie's mother successfully turned the topic of her wedding into a divide-and-conquer smear campaign through social media. Julie sobbed with disbelief each week in my office leading up to her wedding. Her mother threatened all of Julie's extended family on social media, informing them that if they attended Julie's wedding, she would cut them all out of her life. Sadly, very few of Julie's family members attended her wedding, wishing to stay out of the drama.

It was humiliating for Julie to see so many lies posted on social media for everyone, family and nonfamily, to view. It destroyed her to see how much power her mother had over influencing people's decisions, and how cruelly her family behaved over one of the most important and defining moments of her life. This public experience in social media shook her to her core and left her feeling a loss of hope and belief in all people.

Several of Julie's extended family members later lived to regret their participation, but so much damage, humiliation, and abandonment had been inflicted on Julie that their remorse and efforts at apologizing fell painfully short of healing her wounds or repairing those once-close relationships. The best course of action to take when your family abuses you via social media is to block, remove, and delete them from your social media outlets.

Self-Doubt and Anxiety Provoked by Post-Separation Abuse

Post-separation abuse will be a persistent challenge in the aftermath, which makes it easy to understand why survivors are consumed with self-doubt and anxiety, and how and why cutting ties with family, for so many of us, is lived as a silent epidemic. Any conversation about it is painful and triggering. Your family wants you to know they will never give up trying to keep you under their control. In their minds, they will not lose. They will do whatever it takes, by any means possible, to make sure they gain entrance into your life by either being invasive or withholding something important from you. Post-separation abuse is designed to make you doubt yourself, but there are skills you can use to protect yourself against it:

- Accept that you cannot change your family members, but you can change your reaction to them.

- In any potential battle, you must leave your family and their messengers with the shame and humiliation they were trying to impose on you by possessing the insight and poise to walk away in critical moments.

- Let go of any person contributing to your pain. Establish the mindset that if someone or something is not adding more positivity than negativity to your life, you can get rid of it. Otherwise you live life feeling paranoid, never knowing who knows what or what untruths about you must be cleared up, and unable to properly gauge who you can count on.

- Let go of fighting with your family members over issues not reflective of your core values. When your family holds the belief that you need or count on certain relationships, people, or possessions to survive, they believe if they threaten these essential things and relationships, you will acquiesce to them.

It is not your responsibility to make your family members happy. It never was. That type of existence is overly stressful for any person. This pressure to make others happy turns you into a pleaser as an adult. I am sorry that you were made to feel you had to alter who you were to get your basic needs met. Understand that seeking the joy of your own happiness will far outweigh the heavy burden of being held accountable for someone else's.

With these healthy boundaries and this mindset in place, you can seek clarity on who and what is important to you and who and what you need to protect from your family's manipulations. The next chapter offers guidance.

Chapter 16

Protecting Valuable Relationships with Nontoxic Family Members

If you're like many survivors, you have a large family and a host of nontoxic family members or close family friends who are important to you. Understandably, you value your relationships with these healthier family members and would like to protect and preserve them. Unfortunately, navigating these relationships can be confusing and difficult, because any tie back to your family keeps you attached to your trauma. When your healthier family members are aware of the estrangement, and perhaps have a vague knowledge of why you made this decision, it can feel somewhat betraying when these healthier people, for their own reasons, choose to maintain their connection to your abusers. These feelings of betrayal make it difficult to separate your loving feelings for your healthy family members from your painful feelings for your toxic family.

The key issue when establishing and maintaining these relationships is emotional safety. To feel safe with your healthier family members will require your trust. Yet trust will prove to be challenging. Developing or maintaining trust is especially hard when your nontoxic family members bring up the manipulations your toxic family members are currently acting out. Your healthier family members often feel at liberty to share this information because they believe that with your experience you will understand their frustration. Unfortunately, when they share information like this, it gives you the false impression that they are on your side, until you discover in one way or another that they are still in regular contact with your emotionally abusive family.

In these instances, it is hard not to feel feelings of betrayal. Maintaining relationships with your healthier family members is murky and triggering because they are caught in the middle, through no one's fault—theirs or yours. You don't want to be the person putting them in the middle, nor do you want to be in a relationship where you feel paranoid about your toxic family members putting them in the middle. You know how your family is. They will use anyone they can to keep you in the role of the outcast and scapegoat.

The Scapegoat

The moment you choose to sever ties with family, if you weren't already the scapegoat beforehand (though it's likely you were), your decision to cut ties will effectively place you in that role. To be the scapegoat means your family will (or has always) repeatedly cast you in a negative light, portraying who you are to others in a one-dimensional view that denies the fullness of your humanity. The family scapegoat is the person the family labels as mentally ill, emotionally unstable, or a liar.

For example, you may have been labeled "not well"—and in all honesty, if these claims weren't potentially both personally and professionally harmful, they would be laughable. Yet these are the go-to lies your exploitative family members spread to scapegoat you. Naturally, to be spoken about in this way is traumatizing. These lies spread by your family are nothing but defamatory propaganda, but many people, including your healthier family members, will not question or investigate the stories told, nor will they take a stand for you, for fear of getting on your family's bad side. You know there is no truth to your toxic family's disparaging lies, but you are rendered defenseless against them because any reaction you show will be viewed by others as evidence of your mental health problems.

You may have been the scapegoat your entire life. You were that kid who took all the blame, that kid who was labeled bad, that kid your family had to warn people about. You were likely at their disposal to be blamed for their wrongdoings so they could escape responsibility. Every single family member, healthy or not, who knew of the reality behind this scapegoating and did not question it or come to your defense was to some extent a participant in this manipulation against you.

Sadly, you may have believed your family's false narrative. However, you may have found that the more you distanced yourself from your family, the more you distanced yourself from their false narrative of you. This distance likely allowed you to see there was another reality of who you are outside of the one imposed on you since birth.

This new reality can come as quite a shock. What you had always known or felt to be true in your own internal world was in fact the truth. You weren't the mentally ill, horrible person they had you and many others believing you were. Did you struggle as a child? Yes, because you tried to fight for yourself and stand up for what you believed in. Were you being emotionally abused and manipulated? Yes. Did you have a strong reaction to the abuses and manipulations doled out by your family? Probably. Your family likely handled this by turning your fighting for yourself into a grotesque narrative about your poor mental health and instability.

This new reality, the truth you began to learn or are now discovering, is the beginning of the end of your relationships with your coercive family and anyone who supports their propaganda. Your severing ties means you have woken up. Once you discover the truth, it cannot be packed away in a corner of your psyche. The truth is destined to come out. The truth will not allow you to ignore it or forget about it. There is really no way to keep down a truth that demands expression.

When you tell the truth, it will be powerful enough to act as a destabilizing force in a family system that depends on lies, false narratives, control, guilt, denial, and projection to maintain its equilibrium. While the truth is destabilizing to a psychologically abusive family, it will be a stabilizing force for you. A great way to make your truth clear when trying to protect and maintain relationships with your healthier family members is through defining and discussing your nonnegotiables.

Nonnegotiable Boundaries Clear Confusion

Your healthier family members may completely understand your situation or go through a period of trying to get you to reconnect with your family. Your boundaries can break through the confusion. To maintain a healthy relationship with healthier family members, it's important that you set up an agreement that the topic of your toxic family is off limits for discussion. You need to state this boundary as nonnegotiable.

This boundary protects not only you but also all others involved from unhealthy triangulations. Particularly when your healthier family members continue to stay in contact with your toxic family members, you need a boundary around negative gossip about your toxic family that the healthier family members may feel compelled to share. That kind of gossip may be rewarding for your ego, but it's not healthy for your heart. And if your healthier family members share positive things about your family, it will likely be aggravating to hear, not because you wish your family harm but because it reminds you of the estrangement and the abuse that led to it.

Boundaries insulate you from having to explain your feelings, reasonings, and the details of your pain. Unfortunately, the boundaries you set in place with your healthier family members may, for a time, make it feel as if you are ignoring the elephant in the room. It may even feel like your relationship with them will never be fully authentic or transparent because the topic of your family cannot safely be discussed. This is okay. This is simply a period of adjustment. The boundaries you have in place help you define and establish the new normal for these relationships. Adjusting may be uncomfortable at first, but that's par for the course. If there is love there, it will be worth the temporary discomfort. To get through this period of discomfort, focus on applying self-control to your impulses that are driven by curiosity, fear, or anxiety around your family.

Emotional Regulation

Boundaries require you to regulate your emotions by exercising patience and self-control. It will likely be difficult, at first, to not want to know what your healthier family members know about you or your toxic family that you are unaware of. It is normal to feel anxiety that your toxic family members are negatively smearing you to your healthier family members (or have done so in the past) to get them to join the dark side. You are likely right. In psychological warfare, innocent peripheral people are always recruited to join in on the abuse, because abusers are more powerful in numbers.

As we discussed in previous chapters, your family members have no problem trying to force those in the middle to take sides. When you set boundaries, you do not put this same coercive pressure on your healthier family members to take your side, even though you may be tempted to. Your primary job is to exercise self-control over your curiosity about what has been or is being said about you, and to instead focus exclusively on the relationship with the person or people you are still connected with. Understandably, when fear is involved, this is no easy task. It is natural to care about what is being said behind your back, because you will want the chance to correct the false narrative.

To stay in relationships with your healthier family members, it is best to let them have their own experiences of your family. If, however, they confront you with your toxic family's false narrative about you—which would be a major violation of your boundary—you need to remind them that your prohibition of discussion of all topics involving your family is nonnegotiable.

> **Moment of Insight:** Most people will not be able to understand how emotionally incapacitating it is to be the focus of the destructive, degrading, condemning, shaming narrative of a smear campaign.

You can say something like, "Thank you for sharing that. I believe your intentions are good. I just want to remind you that hearing anything about my family, good or bad, is triggering and wounding for me, so I prefer to not hear anything." Resetting these boundaries can certainly bring up fears of conflict, fears of your healthier family members turning against you and scapegoating you as "unreasonable" for reinforcing the boundary. These fears are present because your toxic family has never respected the boundaries you set on them, a circumstance that is largely responsible for your experience of abandonment. Nonetheless, for you to be and feel safe in the relationship with your healthier family members, and for the relationship to work long term, your boundaries must be clear and respected.

Protecting Your Mental Health and Well-Being

Your nonnegotiables are designed to keep the good in and the bad out. These lines of tolerance are direct statements of your self-worth; they define what you will and will not tolerate and serve to protect and insulate your mental and emotional health.

I treat a patient named Taylor; his story is a good illustration.

Taylor was forced to cut ties with his pill-popping, alcoholic, emotionally violent, irresponsible mother. He came into therapy when he realized there was no way for him to be healthy or manage his own issues with addiction as long as his mother continued to overwhelm him with her addiction, threats of suicide, lack of money, and tugging on Taylor to rescue and save her. We talked about boundaries, and he set many, none of which his mother respected. She left him no other option than to sever ties.

Once he severed ties, he felt huge relief and was better able to gain control over his own addictive tendencies that were compromising his work and love life. His life greatly improved. For a time, he was able to maintain a decent and respectful relationship with some of his nontoxic family members as well, specifically his maternal grandmother. Taylor's grandmother agreed that Taylor's mother would not be discussed between the two of them. As time went on, however, his grandmother got loose about respecting Taylor's boundaries, telling Taylor his mother was getting sober, and offering him unwanted detail.

Taylor's mom was able to manipulate his grandmother into getting a card from her to Taylor. The card was sprayed with his mother's perfume and loaded with over-the-top fake sentiment. Taylor instantly saw through her manipulation and immediately reset the boundaries with his grandmother, telling her that giving him this card from his mother only confirmed to him how toxic his mother still was.

Taylor's grandmother didn't like this boundary because it interfered with her hope that her daughter was making real progress. The grandmother intimated to Taylor that his rejection of his mother would cause his mother to relapse. This sent Taylor into a tailspin of guilt and anger.

In therapy, we unpacked his guilt and saw it for what it was. He continued in his commitment to his nonnegotiables, and things were good for a while. However, eventually his grandmother crossed his boundary again by sending Taylor a video his mother had made. In the video, Taylor's mother was slurring her words while talking sobriety. She said if Taylor could just give her a chance it would persuade his siblings to follow suit, and then she would have her life back. The video message was all about her, what she wanted for herself, and how Taylor was the only way she could get it. This again sent Taylor into an emotional downward spiral. He was also angry at his grandmother, though he understood her relentless hope for her daughter, his addict mother. Nevertheless, he engaged with his grandmother to reset his nonnegotiable boundaries, telling her that all topics regarding his mother had to be off the table, and if she could not respect this, it would end their relationship.

Taylor has largely backed away from communication with his grandmother. He's tired of being called insensitive and harsh because he has set healthy boundaries.

Moment of Insight: Of course you're angry. You were abused by family members with no conscience or remorse. And when you reached out for help, you were judged and shamed for speaking out, and people supported your abusers instead.

Remember, you have every right to put your mental health above all else in the relationships you choose to have with your healthier family members.

It is painful to face these moments of conflict and to have to set and reset boundaries with your healthier family members. It is hard, from your perspective, to understand when they forget or seemingly don't understand the depth of your pain. They don't seem to understand that time doesn't heal the pain of your family wound. What does help you heal is setting boundaries. Boundaries are your saving grace. Time and space certainly help ease your everyday emotional pain, but they are not a cure. There is no cure. However, when the boundaries you set are upheld and respected by your healthier family members, loving relationships with them are absolutely possible.

Coping with Unwanted Incidental Situations

It is important to prepare for unexpected and unwanted ways you will hear information about your toxic family via your healthier family members but not directly from them. When you spend time around your healthier family members, this almost always means you will also be around their children and their other extended family, such as cousins and in-laws, and perhaps their group of friends. If your healthier family members or close family friends are in regular contact with your family, they're likely to mention unwanted information about your family in conversations. You may hear their children or other connections talking about having seen your family recently. These situations tend to stir up a host of painful and uncomfortable emotions. First, none of your boundaries have been directly crossed by the healthy family members you have established boundaries with. Further, your healthier family members have very little control over the conversations at these gatherings, and word of your toxic family members may accidentally come up. It is not reasonable to have your healthier family members walking on eggshells trying to quash and control all such conversations.

In these scenarios it's most important, again, to regulate your emotions—managing your emotional state in a way that is adaptable, flexible, and tolerant. Being in these uncomfortable situations helps you develop resiliency. It is an excellent time to practice being a great listener, to restrain your impulse to say something when the topic of your family comes up, and to practice being accepting of people who choose to have relationships with them. Most people would never know the deep levels of toxicity that exist in your family unless they were raised with them. It is not your duty to protect anyone else from their manipulation. Your job is to protect yourself and allow everyone else to learn on their own.

Consider what level of contact is the most healthy way to interact with nontoxic family members.

- *High contact.* High contact can be successful with your healthier family members when they respect and uphold the boundaries you've set around discussing your toxic family. You can then feel safe in these relationships, which allows you to spend as much time around them as you desire without keeping your self-protective guard up.

- *Low contact.* With some healthier family members, you may not feel completely safe. In these relationships, you may keep having to set and reset your boundaries around discussing your family. With low contact, you can be in contact and even spend time with them. But the more superficial you can keep these relationships, the lower the likelihood that your boundaries will be crossed.

- *Cordial contact.* You have limited or minimal contact with these nontoxic family members because too often they have been unable to be respectful or understanding of your boundaries. These are the people who are happy to be in the middle and to pass gossip both ways. It is best to see these people as little as possible. If you do run into them, be cordial but know the limits of conversation and time spent with them that you can safely participate in.

- *No contact.* These are family members who are also toxic. They have likely made efforts and/or judgments to bully you back into the relationship with your abusive family members. These relationships are neither safe nor respectful. They are harmful and have no business being a part of your life.

The only true responsibility you have in your relationships is for your own mental health. It is your job to take care of yourself for other people, and it is their job to take care of themselves for you. In your own life, you must put your mental health first. Keep in mind that you are a cycle breaker. You are wise enough to recognize that you have the potential to be just as cruel and manipulative as your family has been toward you, but you're empathetic enough to sacrifice your familiarity with that type of abuse in order to break the cycle. You do this through setting boundaries.

With ties severed and strict boundaries placed on your family, the next step on your journey is learning to fully rely upon yourself.

Conclusion

The Liberation of Self-Reliance

It is time to master being your own person. No more manipulation, no more confusion, no more guilt. Just the freedom that comes with self-reliance. This freedom allows you to redefine the landscape of your life and personality without a coercive family pulling you away from yourself. When you are free to hold and embrace your own opinions, beliefs, and feelings apart from the family who manipulated and abused you, you quickly become self-defined. When you are self-defined, you recognize that you are responsible for determining and evaluating your worth and progress as a person. Your worth is no longer determined by others or society. Welcome to self-reliance!

Here are some things you can give yourself, never having to rely on anyone else to bestow—or withhold—them again:

- Reliance on common sense

- Mastery of everyday life skills

- Maintenance of your self-worth

- Ability to make your own decisions

- The right to hold your own opinions

- Responsibility for taking care of your health

Self-reliance is marked by your ability to draw upon your own strength to live your life well. Living with emptiness where the presence of family should be is like trying to breathe at high elevation. Your body adapts to the thin air, but it has to work much harder to survive. As you become more and more self-reliant, your living style will adapt to the emptiness of family in your life.

We're now going to explore some mindfulness techniques to help aid you in embracing the gifts that being self-reliant offers. To become self-reliant, practice the following:

- *Embrace self-sufficiency.* Take full responsibility for the quality of your thoughts, feelings, and emotions. In cutting ties, you have made a commitment to preserve your mental health and wellness by not running back to your toxic family members in your weaker, more vulnerable moments. You choose to count on yourself and other helpful, healthy, supportive others.

- *Control your own life decisions.* You are the person who has the authority to make choices about your future. Whether that feels exciting or intimidating, the power is now with you. Severing ties gives you the authority to have the final say on anything and everything in your life. Decision making means you say no when you need to say no, and yes when you want to say yes.

- *Develop new life skills.* Being self-reliant allows you to develop the skills and resourcefulness needed to live with maturity, security, and peace. When you need help and are being challenged, you should feel no shame in asking for support. Part of being self-reliant is asking for help when you need it.

Moment of Insight: The greatest payback for your toxic family members is your inner peace, your happiness, and a beautifully flourishing life.

- *Master emotional regulation.* The more in tune you are with your feelings, thoughts, and emotions, the less power they will have to overwhelm and incapacitate you. To be self-reliant, learn to take a moment before reacting. When you are in control of your reactions, you will establish mastery in your relationships.

- *Protect your peace.* When you take the time to connect with your emotional well-being, you can give attention to the things that don't feel right, and determine if they need to be removed from your life. Your boundaries act as your peacekeepers.

- *Check in with yourself.* One of the easiest ways to gauge your emotional temperature is to ask yourself, *How am I doing? Am I happy?* This attentive questioning puts you in touch with what is going on inside. Once you know how you are doing, you can either do things to improve your state of mind or relax, knowing you are doing just fine.

- *Stop comparing yourself to others.* Feeling good enough comes from within. Look inward for approval and validation. It is a great practice to make a list of the qualities you possess that make you exceptional. On down days, you can refer to your list of exceptional qualities and allow these "brag moments" to shift your state of mind back to reality—to the phenomenal person you are.

- *Trust your instincts.* You likely have well-developed intuitive skills to accurately interpret the emotional climate of your relationships. This is an incredible asset that allows you to more fully rely on yourself. When you sense that someone may be toxic, that feeling will rarely be wrong. Learn to trust yourself.

Make the Choice to Live Each Day Better Than the One Before

The more you love and nurture your heart, mind, and body, the more confidence you will develop and the more love and abundance you will attract into your life. When you love the person in the mirror, whether your toxic family loved that person or not, it will inspire you to take the necessary steps to live your life as you see fit. Self-reliance means you trust you are someone you can count on.

Moment of Insight: Trust yourself. Be the kind of person you will be happy to live with all your life.

Holding this mindset will help you cope. Life will always bring the unexpected. Your deeper wounds are always active and will be fairly easy to trigger. This can be a great gift if you choose to look at it that way. The more open you are to healing, the better you can cope with life's unexpected events.

Embrace Unexpected Healing Moments

In the aftermath of cutting ties, and for the remainder of your life, you will run into some beautiful but unexpected moments that push your pain to the surface, when your trauma does not feel old, but rather fresh, as if the original wound happened yesterday. These moments deepen your ability to rely on yourself.

I experienced a moment like this watching the band the X Ambassadors at the Grammy Museum in Los Angeles. One of the songs they sang was a stripped-down version of "Unsteady." I encourage you to listen to it. When the lead singer introduced it, he shared that the song was about devotion, because as band members they were unconditionally devoted to each other, like family. It struck me that toxic families have no sense of loving *devotion* toward each other. What I heard in the lyrics was a child pleading for his toxic family to be healthy, to show up for him and hold on to him so that he could feel steady.

At the concert, the word "unsteady" suddenly hit like a lightning strike, exposing my hurt places. Regardless of how steady my world may look or even how steady I have created it to be, there are still moments when I feel unsteady. I have never lived a day in this life not feeling nervous. It is a perpetual feeling of waiting for the bottom to fall out. This is C-PTSD, because in truth, my bottom, my foundation, did fall out. For most people the top, the bottom, the up, the down, the left, the right, the very fabric of life that sustains, protects, and stands by them forever, is family. Hearing, in the closing line of the song, the pleading message for a love that doesn't let go was another affirmation of the reality—my reality and yours—that our family never "loved" in a way where we felt held or safe.

Through all this, I had that uncomfortable feeling of warmth in my body that occurs when my vulnerabilities are rising to the surface. I tensed up, trying to block the emotions that were coming, because I was in a public place. My tears came anyway. In all honesty, it is not easy for me to cry for myself—I reason this is because I never felt loved enough to be cried for. Amazingly, the sweetest woman sitting next to me, who was a complete stranger, sensed my emotion and placed her hand on my shoulder for the remainder of the song. I acknowledged her empathy and kindness by touching her hand. We were no longer strangers in that moment but two human beings connecting in a shared experience. I am happy she was there.

> **Take a Moment for You:** Reflect on songs or other types of movement, cinema, or art that you can bring to your wound. If you can identify these, what are they, and how do they validate you?

At the concert, I became acutely aware that the loss of family is past, present, and future: it is in the past that the pain of feeling unwanted began; in the present moment, that the post-separation abuse and abandonment continue; and in the future that there is no projected hope for connection, love, or resolution.

Be Patient with the Process of Healing

There is a big difference between healing and being healed. As you continue to learn to fully rely on yourself in a healthy way, it's important to accept that you will be in the process of healing for the remainder of your life. After severing ties with your family, being fully "healed" is not a reality you can expect. However, this in no way makes you doomed; rather, it makes you deep. I can say that healing, although painful, is the most interesting, motivating, and inspiring part of my life. It is what my life and purpose function around: the hows, the whys, and the whats of who I am and the path that brought me to be this person, helping others to do the same. I view healing as a verb, forever in action.

Take a Moment for You: Reflect on how or whether you can turn your healing journey into your redemptive passion.

Avoid the Victim Mentality

To become self-reliant, avoid allowing yourself to be the victim. This is not to say you have not been horribly victimized. One is in the present moment (victim) and one is in the past (victimized). One is permanent (victim) and the other, transformative (victimized). One is the caterpillar (victim); the other is the butterfly (victimized). You may have been victimized as recently as yesterday, but as the butterfly, it's still in the past, and you are coming out of that chrysalis using every ounce of information and detail you can gather from your victimization to make this knowledge useful in your life.

The goal is to turn the inescapable reality of your perpetrators into a positive purpose. You cannot gain traction in your life if you commit to staying within your chrysalis. Keep in mind that bitterness does not and will not change your pain. Here is what I know for sure: complaining about your circumstances does not change them, fearing them does not transform them, not liking them does not make them better, resenting them does not vindicate them, and avoiding them does not make the reality of your trauma disappear. Therefore, whenever your abusive family members strike, sting, and hurt you in the aftermath, you must keep moving. You must examine and understand the impact their current strike has on you and take in the lesson. You must allow these experiences to deepen your capacity to rely on yourself.

Are You Getting Any Better?

You may question, *Am I even getting better? Am I always going to have these triggers to my family?* Yes, you are getting better, and yes, there will always be triggers. Therefore, I suggest letting go of any expectation of reaching an end date of being healed. The loss of family is just this monumental. There is nothing wrong with owning the reality of this. Just because you carry the hurt of your scars does not mean you are failing to move forward or that you are not doing your work. You simply move through life with these issues on deck. It would be wonderful if you could delete your experiences and move on as if they never happened, but that is not how being human works.

> **Moment of Insight:** Closure does not come from not feeling the pain anymore. Closure comes from actively healing your pain.

Your healing comes through understanding, and understanding comes though feeling and examining. This is how the process will always be. I can guarantee that the more you heal, educate yourself, understand, and look inside, the more adept you'll become in managing your emotional pain and disappointment over the course of time. The more wisdom you develop, the more connected you'll feel to yourself and others. As you heal, you'll develop a more realistic hope for the potential of who you are in the process of becoming free from the family environment that damaged you.

Most people have their family as the platform they function from and return to for support. You do not. Those of us who are estranged need to do life a bit differently, but that doesn't mean we can't be just as healthy as or healthier than others—even healthier than those who have come from healthier backgrounds. Why? Because you have found your way into self-reliance on your own.

> **Moment of Insight:** Wisdom is what pain looks like when it is healed.

The healing you engage in places a solid platform of focus beneath you, helping you to manage your foundational anxiety. Your foundation is now defined by your commitment to heal, rather than by the family who raised you. This commitment is much steadier than the abusive foundation you came from. Being invested in your personal growth shifts your mindset away from trying to fit into the craziness of your family and toward the steadiness of your growth process. The way the process of healing works is, it waxes and wanes; but I can assure you, the more you heal, the further away from self-doubt and toxic shame you will move, and the more deeply you can trust in and depend upon yourself.

Letting Go of Revenge

As your feelings of frustration, pain, and revulsion for your family decrease in power, you will see that you feel more alive than ever before. Luckily, you've likely already figured out that revenge does not work on your family members anyway. They thrive in the areas of conflict, where they are certain to win. But don't punish yourself for having feelings of wanting revenge. It is natural and even healthy to daydream about exacting revenge on the family who has hurt you so deeply. In fact, I suggest you daydream away!

I can say that my revenge daydreams—imagining my family members feeling as hurt as they made me feel—have been helpful for me. It feels balancing. However, the fault I have noticed in my own daydreaming is that I envision my family actually feeling the pain they have caused me, understanding it, and then showing remorse for what they have done. Unfortunately, these things do not often happen in real life. Nonetheless, daydreaming can be healing, because daydreams can bring you to some sense of closure, while realizing that revenge is not a workable solution if you genuinely want to move forward in your life. Revenge is about looking backward rather than forward. If you are looking backward for healing, your healing will be dependent on something external to you. When you trust that you can rely on yourself, you will trust that healing is always in front of you, not behind you.

Center your life on discovering and creating the happiness you desire and deserve. If you seek revenge, you are still dependent on getting some type of reaction from your family that will satisfy you. When you are focused on your happiness and moving forward, your only focus is on *you* counting on *yourself* to get to where *you* want to be.

Redemption Versus Revenge

Redemption is the rise of the underdog, in which the scapegoated, bullied person achieves greatness regardless of the obstacles their destructive family has generously and strategically placed in their way. The greatest redemption you have is severing ties—taking away from your family their power to manipulate, damage, and control your life.

Redemption is internal (about you), not external (about them). Redemption is that feeling of satisfaction that arises from your own personal development. This is when the fog of the fear-based confusion common to the toxic family system clears, and miracles begin to happen in your life.

I can say that life has gotten staggeringly better since separating myself from my family, because it has given me the faculties I have needed to recover. As I heal, my life heals. Every new great gift, miracle, or opportunity that comes into my life gives me that feeling of redemption: that my pain has been seen, that I have been heard and understood by something somewhere. And so have you. It is that feeling of knowing your voice does have an influence. I now use my voice as a vehicle to add value to the lives of others. I have been blessed with the opportunity to put these words to paper; to share my story, knowledge, education, experience, and research, with the most beautiful, yearning, and deserving hearts that want to heal through what is being offered here. I may not have mattered in my own family, but I matter in this world, and so do you. The greatest redemption is to keep our eye on the ball. Focus on yourself, the goals you want to achieve, and the life you choose to create.

Empower Yourself

Taking charge of your life is empowering. When there are no longer destructive family members chipping away at your self-worth, your decisions, or your emotions, you have the emotional and mental space necessary to feel joyful, to be creative, to be unburdened, and most important, to feel a sense of peace. It is your turn. No more waiting, no more pleasing, no more worrying, and no more operating from shame, guilt, or obligation. You have the potential to amaze yourself with just how capable and powerful you are. You have proven to be strong enough to cut ties with your very foundation. There is nothing more powerful than that. You can feel the comfort of knowing you have already completed the hardest part of the journey. There will never be a more challenging or more significant group of people you will have to remove from your life.

There are special things about you as a person—which you share with all of those who have had to cut ties—that you radiate out into this world and deserve to be proud of:

- You are brave enough to face the truth.

- You are brave enough to tell the truth.

- You are willing to do the arduous emotional work to find yourself.

- You are highly sensitive to the needs of others.

- You trust that your feelings will lead you to a healthier place.

- You choose peace over problems.

- You trust your instincts.

- You see through lies, coverups, and a lack of follow-through.

- You are no longer a pleaser.

- You set healthy boundaries.

- You have a huge, empathic heart.

- You desire to help other people.

- You are brave.

- You are self-reliant.

It is not selfish, nor is it wrong or egotistical to feel good about who you are and the decisions you've made to gain a sense of safety and positive emotional traction. You have had to be courageous. Courage is not so much forced on you anymore as it was when you were being raised; rather, courage has become an integral part of your character. People will sense your courage without even having to know your story. When you are true to yourself, people experience that to be courageous. You can embrace your willingness to be unpopular with your family to remain true to yourself.

Free at Last

As a survivor, you were strong enough to bear the brunt of the dysfunction of your family; therefore you must take moments to admire your strength. Not only did your family not break you, but without knowing it, you also used them to train your toughness, your ability to manage emotional pain and be strong enough to eventually set yourself free from their negative influence. In truth, you turned the tables on them. They mistakenly viewed your sensitivity and willingness to please them to secure their love as a weakness they could control. They were naïve enough to believe you would never seek answers outside of their rule and domination and one day emancipate yourself. But you did! Congratulations! This is a monumental accomplishment.

One woman who saw an advertisement for my first book on Instagram said, "Wow! I have to read this book. Thank you for being courageous enough to write it and share it with the world because so many of us are in that place and fear the outcome or backlash of letting go. I can't wait to read it." Another person who responded to the same advertisement said, "I need to read this. It's comforting to know you're not alone in breaking the toxic cycle." You are *not* alone. (Perhaps as survivors we should start the #NotAlone movement and find each other.)

In making my private life and research public, I am doing this for you. Writing my books has no outward benefit for me, as it only serves to make my family even angrier and more spiteful toward me. I write my books to give you permission to set yourself free. Unencumbered by a controlling and manipulative family, just think of how well your ability to tolerate and intuit people will help you in the world. There is good when you look for it. I would not be me—the woman writing this book, helping people all over the world, while continually healing myself—if I had had any semblance of a different life. I am making the difference in the lives of others that I so desperately needed for someone, anyone, to make in mine.

It brings me joy to give what I never got and to think of how many of you, my readers, feel normal and sane after reading my books. To think of how many of you feel heard, loved, and understood by at least someone; that perhaps you now know you are not alone. Someone is listening. I am listening. I have given the silent epidemic of severing ties with toxic family a voice. Had you come from a different family background, yes, you might have experienced less pain, but you would also have less depth, knowledge, and insight. Grab these gifts and use them for all they are worth. You do not need to credit your toxic family members or their abuses for the successes you have achieved in your life. You need to give all the credit to yourself for overcoming them.

I credit you and admire you.

Acknowledgments

I would like to thank my amazing team at New Harbinger Publications for their belief in this book. So many adult survivors of toxic families feel isolated and alone. I am thankful to have found a publisher brave enough to bring this silent epidemic out of the dark and into the light for conversation and healing, and to encourage people to make family abuse stop with them.

I want to offer a special thank-you to both Jennifer Holder and Elizabeth Hollis Hansen for helping me make this book the best it could be. I enjoyed the editing process and conversation with you both. Both of you made me feel a true and genuine connection to both myself and my message, and I feel that together we are offering an incredible guide to all of those who read these pages. Thank you for your commitment, time, and heartfelt dedication to my message.

I would like to acknowledge my dysfunctional family, for without the exact life I had I would not be the person I am today, whom I can look at in the mirror and genuinely love. Your lack of love for me forced me to learn to love myself, and for that I am thankful.

To my friends and loved ones: Thank you for having my back through thick and thin. Thank you for giving me the room, patience, and space that was and continues to be necessary for me to grieve and grow. Your love for me lifts me up and reminds me that I am lovable. These reminders are vital, for my connections with you are healing to my soul.

The greatest and most heartfelt thank-you goes to my daughter, London. There are no words to express the love I feel for you, and how much having you in my life has inspired me to never do to you what was done to me. There is no manipulation, babygirl. Love is the only language we speak. I have loved and will continue to love and treasure every second you are in my life.

Endnotes

1 Susan Adcox, "What Is Family Estrangement?" (n.d.), https://www
.verywellfamily.com/breakdown-of-family-estrangement-1695444.

2 Shahida Arabi, *Healing the Adult Children of Narcissists: Essays on the
Invisible War Zone* (SCW Archer Publishing, 2019).

3 Stand Alone, "Hidden Voices: Family Estrangement in Adulthood,"
University of Cambridge (n.d.), http://standalone.org.uk/wp-content
/uploads/2015/12/HiddenVoices.-Press.pdf.

4 Ibid.

5 Henry Cloud and John Townsend, *Boundaries: When to Say Yes,
How to Say No, to Take Control of Your Life* (Grand Rapids, MI:
Zondervan, 1992, 2017), 37, 40.

6 Ibid.

7 Sandra Restrepo, dir., *Brené Brown: The Call to Courage*
(Netflix documentary, 2019).

8 Susan Forward, *Toxic Parents: Overcoming Their Hurtful Legacy
and Reclaiming Your Life* (New York: Bantam, 1990).

9 Kendra Cherry, "Erik Erikson's Stages of Psychosocial Development,"
VeryWell Mind (2020, June 16), https://www.verywellmind.com
/erik-eriksons-stages-of-psychosocial-development-795740/.

10 Forward, *Toxic Parents*.

11 Ibid..

12 Regina Sullivan and Elizabeth Norton Lasley, "Fear in Love:
Attachment, Abuse, and the Developing Brain," *Cerebrum*

(2010, September), https://www.ncbi.nlm.nih.gov/pmc/articles /PMC3574772/?report=classic.

13 Bessel van der Kolk, *The Body Keeps the Score: Brain, Mind, and Body in the Healing of Trauma* (New York: Penguin Books, 2014).

14 Ibid., 133.

15 Cherry, "Erik Erikson's Stages of Psychosocial Development."

16 Pete Walker, *Complex PTSD: From Surviving to Thriving: A Guide and Map for Recovering from Childhood Trauma* (Lafayette, CA: Azure Coyote, 2013).

17 Tara Westover, *Educated* (New York: Random House, 2018).

18 Brené Brown, *Braving the Wilderness: The Quest for True Belonging and the Courage to Stand Alone* (New York: Random House, 2017).

19 Susan Anderson, *The Journey from Abandonment to Healing: Turn the End of a Relationship into the Beginning of a New Life* (New York: Berkeley Books, 2014).

20 Ibid.

21 Shannon Thomas, *Exposing Financial Abuse: When Money Is a Weapon* (New York: MAST Publishing House, 2018), 4.

22 H. G. Tudor, *Manipulated* (Oklahoma City: Insight Books, 2015).

Sherrie Campbell, PhD, is a licensed psychologist who specializes in helping healthy people cut ties with the toxic people in their lives. She is a nationally recognized expert on family estrangement, an inspirational speaker, former radio host of the *Dr. Sherrie Show* on BBM Global Network and Tune-In Radio, a social media influencer, and a regularly featured media expert.

Foreword writer **Wendy T. Behary, LCSW**, is founder and clinical director of The Cognitive Therapy Center of New Jersey, founding fellow of the Academy of Cognitive Therapy, and author *Disarming the Narcissist*.

Real change *is* possible

For more than forty-five years, New Harbinger has published proven-effective self-help books and pioneering workbooks to help readers of all ages and backgrounds improve mental health and well-being, and achieve lasting personal growth. In addition, our spirituality books offer profound guidance for deepening awareness and cultivating healing, self-discovery, and fulfillment.

Founded by psychologist Matthew McKay and Patrick Fanning, New Harbinger is proud to be an independent, employee-owned company. Our books reflect our core values of integrity, innovation, commitment, sustainability, compassion, and trust. Written by leaders in the field and recommended by therapists worldwide, New Harbinger books are practical, accessible, and provide real tools for real change.

newharbingerpublications

MORE BOOKS from
NEW HARBINGER PUBLICATIONS

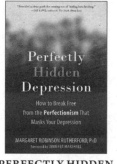
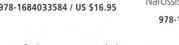

Did you know there are **free tools** you can download for this book?

Free tools are things like **worksheets**, **guided meditation exercises**, and **more** that will help you get the most out of your book.

You can download free tools for this book—whether you bought or borrowed it, in any format, from any source—from the New Harbinger website. All you need is a NewHarbinger.com account. Just use the URL provided in this book to view the free tools that are available for it. Then, click on the "download" button for the free tool you want, and follow the prompts that appear to log in to your NewHarbinger.com account and download the material.

You can also save the free tools for this book to your **Free Tools Library** so you can access them again anytime, just by logging in to your account! Just look for this button on the book's free tools page.

+ Save this to my free tools library

If you need help accessing or downloading free tools, visit **newharbinger.com/faq** or contact us at **customerservice@newharbinger.com**.